I like this book by A. L. Williams. Surprising results are achieved when you do *all* you *can*. This book really motivated me. I think it's great!

Dr. Norman Vincent Peale

Art Williams has done it again! In this book he shows that he has the great sensitivity to people and the perceptiveness to business which have made him so successful over the years. I think he's ready for a trip to the moon!

Alan Shepard
Astronaut

Faith remains the most dynamic and energizing force. But winning also requires effort and strategy. Art Williams has the formula.

Gary Player
World Renowned Professional Golfer

AYCDIAYCD gives straight talk on winning from a proven winner. Art Williams has, against all odds, challenged one of the most competitive industries in this country and has built one of the most successful companies of our day. This is great reading for anyone in any walk of life who wants to win. AYCDIAYCD is a textbook for success.

Rev. Jerry Falwell

Art Williams is a true winner. He's the kind of guy you want on the mound in the 7th game of the World Series. Anyone who reads this book will get a lesson in winning.

Whitey Ford
Former Pitcher, New York Yankees

Art Williams is right: There's only one way to become a champ—master the fundamentals.

Rocky Graziano
Middleweight Boxing Champion of the World

If anybody knows about winning, and how to help others win, it's Art Williams. He coached kids to win in football, and now he coaches adults to win in their professional pursuits. I've written about winning myself, and I know a winner when I see one: Congratulations to Art Williams, a winner materially, emotionally, and spiritually. What else is there?

Pat Boone

With so much talk recently of America's loss of stature in the world, it is refreshing to read something that fosters positive thinking and a self-assuredness that have long been hallmarks of our country's greatness. It is an inspiration to all managers and a pleasure to read.

John B. Curcio
Chairman and CEO, Mack Trucks, Inc.

Art Williams' book AYCDIAYCD touches *all* the bases. Down to earth and practical, it is an inspiring message of hope built on timeless principles and procedures—solid help for anyone interested in a higher quality of life.

Zig Ziglar

Art Williams' life is a true American success story. As someone who never went to college and doesn't have a high-school diploma, I can join him in celebrating this unique country of ours in which hard work can propel one to successes unimagined in other countries. Everyone should pay special attention to his story.

Ambassador Vernon A. Walters
United States' Permanent Representative
to the United Nations

Art Williams is a human dynamo. I wish he worked for our company.

Don Tyson
Chairman and CEO, Tyson Foods Inc.

AYCDIAYCD is an exciting confirmation of what people can accomplish when they know what they want and go after it.

Cory SerVaas, M.D.
Editor, The Saturday Evening Post

Art Williams' new book, AYCDIAYCD, is another way of saying that success in life is not relative to anything except one's self. The book is well worth reading for aspiring young people.

Jack Stephens
Chairman of the Board, Stephens Inc.

Art Williams has established a simple formula for success. His priorities and philosophy are much akin to my own. Reading his book and applying its principles will certainly have a positive influence on the reader.

S. Truett Cathy
Founder and Chairman, Chick-fil-A, Inc.

Anyone interested in truly succeeding—succeeding in business, succeeding in life—will find Art Williams' book a true revelation. Art lives his beliefs. Art believes in his work. If you study Art's principles and apply them to your life, they will help you find true happiness and true success.

Honorable Newt Gingrich
United States Congress

A. L. (Art) Williams has shown through this book that positive thinking and positive action is the formula for a positive life. This is a powerful step by step guide to success, and should be on everyone's reading list.

Max Cleland
Secretary of State, State of Georgia

The Bible's teaching, "Whatever a man sows, that he will also reap" (Galatians 6:7 NKJV), is amply demonstrated in this book. Whether it be an investment of time, talent, or treasure, if we give it "all we can do," it should prove to be enough. It is also emphasized that success, for fame or fortune or merely for the sake of being considered successful, is not enough. To be really successful, due consideration must also be given to helping others along the way. You will find the book AYCDIAYCD to be highly motivational and well worth your reading.

Dr. Bill Bright
Founder and President,
Campus Crusade for Christ International

A great motivational story told in simplistic terms, built around a business and sports environment. Recommended reading and reflection for all but the chosen few who have experienced and been successful with the commitment, crusade, and wisdom of the author.

Raymond A. Mueller
Chairman, Comair, Inc.

As a Christian pastor who interacts daily with highly motivated business people, this is one book which I will gladly recommend. AYCDIAYCD is delightful. Williams has loaded this practical book with illustrations that lifted my vision beyond the mundane.

As a Christian, I believe my responsibility is to be hope personified in this world. There are numerous depictions of hope in his book. His optimism is not of the cotton-candy variety. Williams' feet are solidly planted on this planet. Anyone who daily confronts goals and objectives will benefit by reading this book.

Rev. David G. McKechnie
Pastor, Grace Presbyterian Church, Houston, Texas

ALL YOU CAN DO
is
ALL YOU CAN DO

but all you can do is enough!

ALL YOU CAN DO
is
ALL YOU CAN DO

*but all you can do is
enough!*

A. L. WILLIAMS

OLIVER
NELSON

A Division of Thomas Nelson Publishers

NASHVILLE

Published in Nashville, Tennessee, by Oliver-Nelson Books, a division of Thomas Nelson, Inc., Publishers, and distributed in Canada by Lawson Falle, Ltd., Cambridge, Ontario.

The Scripture verse in Chapter 9 is taken from *The Living Bible*, Copyright 1971 by Tyndale House Publishers, Wheaton, IL. Used by permission.

Printed in the United States of America.

Library of Congress
Library of Congress Cataloging-in-Publication Data

Williams, Art.
    All you can do is all you can do, but all you can do is enough
A.L. Williams.
        p.   cm.
    ISBN 0-8407-9010-4   : $14.95
    1. Success in business.   I. Title.
HF5386.W498   1988
650.1—dc19   88-18022
                                                                              CIP

4 5 6—93 92 91 90 89 88

To my Angela.
She caught my eye in the second grade
and has held my heart ever since.
She is the most perfect wife
God ever gave a man.

All royalties from this book will be donated to A. L. Williams Family and Marriage Resources in the name of Angela Hancock Williams. She is the inspiration behind the program—a nonprofit organization helping business people find success at home *and* in the workplace—and I can think of no greater way to honor her.

Contents

Foreword

This is a book about America's ladder of opportunity, a real success story. It shows how, after two hundred years, the American pioneering spirit still lives, and still energizes our society.

This is a book about Americans themselves—not the blue bloods, the highbrows, and those who got their money the old-fashioned way (by inheriting it)—the common and not-so-common. It is about people who were programmed to believe that "average" was the best they could hope for but who still gained success, people who may have been born on the "wrong side of the tracks" yet ended up with enough wealth to buy the railroad.

And, finally, this is a book about an individual American, a real person who not only shows us how to scale the ladder of opportunity but who also demonstrates through vision, courage, and determination how you can add new rungs to the ladder.

The individual is Arthur Lynch Williams, or simply "Art," as most people know him.

I first met Art Williams during my second term as President of the National Association of Consumer Agency Administrators, a position I held while also serving as the head of Georgia's Consumer Protection Agency. By this time Art was already a multimillionaire, but I would never have guessed if someone had not already told me. His unpretentious demeanor was disarming; his wrinkled white shirt, loosened tie, and casual slacks were not the dress-for-success look then—and now—in vogue; and his open, warm manner was quite different from the more aloof, guarded style I had experienced in dealing with other corporate leaders.

"You and I both want what's best for the consumer," he

said. Coming from a businessman, this was greeted initially with the skepticism one might expect from a consumer advocate. But time, experience, and knowledge about A. L. Williams soon erased my skepticism.

In the same conversation he told me his company, A. L. Williams, would soon overtake Prudential in life insurance sales. I thought to myself, "You are going to take on one of the largest, oldest, crustiest, most established industries with more than 2,000 companies in it and turn it topsy-turvy by knocking off Number One? Good Luck!"

But, guess what? Today A. L. Williams is outselling not only Prudential, but several of the largest life insurance companies *combined*. The face amount of individual life insurance sold by A. L. Williams in 1987 was a staggering $81 billion (Prudential had $26.5 billion), a total far outstripping companies whose names have been household words since the life insurance industry began.

It all started in 1977 when Art—a successful football coach turned successful salesman turned company executive—joined with eighty-five other people to establish their own company. Many of this group of eighty-five, like Art, had once been teachers and high-school coaches. In their beginnings, they had all the marks of being long shots in pursuit of success.

Rejecting all conventional wisdom about how to make it big in insurance, they decided to sell term insurance and investments. Eventually, this idea would revolutionize the life insurance industry that for decades has fed off consumer confusion about life insurance.

They believed in the American Dream of individual success. They wanted to own their own business, build a company in which they could call the shots, and earn financial independence for their families.

The dream delivered. In early 1988, A. L. Williams had over five hundred people earning six-figure incomes and more bona fide millionaires than any other ten-year-old company.

In addition, A. L. Williams is now the world's largest financial services marketing organization, a dynamic network of people stretching across the U.S. from Canada to Puerto Rico to Guam, and a success story without parallel.

Is A. L. Williams something you can share in? Are there lessons in the A. L. Williams story that can help you in your business or profession? Yes. In this book you will find A. L. Williams's secrets to winning. They include philosophies Art Williams has cultivated and stuck with all of his life. In reading his simply expressed, straightforward thoughts and illustrations, you will see that, like a modern-day Thomas Edison, he is creative. He is an inventor of ways to win for people typically locked out of corporate America. And like Henry Ford, he has relentlessly pursued a goal of bringing opportunity and hope to Middle America.

Two notes of caution before you read further: *First,* this is not a get-rich-quick recipe book. Although the writing freely uses sports analogies and examples, Art Williams doesn't go for the one big play. Rather, his philosophy of success is one in which you methodically slug it out, stick to the game plan, think winning thoughts, and execute! execute! execute! *Second,* this book may not be for everyone. It contains dangerous ideas about who can be a winner in America.

And you know what? The ideas are highly contagious. So, get ready to change your whole life when you delve into Chapter 1.

TIM RYLES, PH.D.
Consumer Affairs Specialist

Introduction

Do you know these people?

They come from a privileged background. They're the "elite" of society. Their parents are college-educated, professional people. They've gone to the best Ivy League schools—probably Harvard or Yale.

They're tall, slim, handsome. They wear those beautiful tailored suits with the latest "power" ties.

They have perfect teeth and beautiful smiles and charismatic personalities that earn instant respect and admiration.

They succeed at everything they do, from tennis to business.

They have magazine-cover wives and perfect children.

Everything about them is perfect.

I'm sure you recognize these people. You've probably even known some. They're the *lucky* people, the world's success stories. You just know they're going to be somebody, even when they're young, because they're the people who are *supposed* to be successful.

But you know what's discouraging about that picture?

Those people are nothing like you and me.

Let me paint you a different picture. Imagine a guy who's kind of short. He looks very ordinary; if you saw him on the street, nothing would make you turn and stare. He looks sort of like you do—just an average guy. His hair is turning a little grey—what is left of it, which isn't too much. He's always watching his weight because he loves to eat, especially sweets. He's in good shape, but you wouldn't find him in a Mr. Universe contest. He was an average student, not very good in math, a terrible speller. He comes from an average family and was born and reared in a little town in south Georgia. He was a fair high-school athlete, but he doesn't even know how to play tennis.

You know that person, too, don't you?

He's not nearly as exciting as the first people I described, but you feel a little more comfortable with him, right? He probably sounds a little bit more like somebody you know pretty well—yourself.

But you know what? The guy I just described—Art Williams—runs one of the fastest-growing companies in America today, a company with over $81 *billion* of individual life insurance placed in force in 1987 and offices in forty-nine states, Puerto Rico, Guam, and Canada. He started his own company at age thirty-three and became a millionaire at age thirty-seven. His company, A. L. Williams, has produced more executives with six-figure incomes and more millionaires in its ten-year history than any company in American business.

How can that be? How did somebody like me, who only a few years ago was a football coach in Columbus, Georgia, making $10,700 a year, ever "make it" in corporate America?

That's what this book is all about. It's a book about winning by a man who wasn't supposed to win. I thought about calling it *How to Win—if You Look Like I Do.*

Who said Art Williams wasn't supposed to win? Well, just about everybody. Society, my friends and neighbors, even some of my relatives. Most important, I agreed with them. Where I came from, people like Art Williams didn't become millionaires; they didn't drive big cars and run giant corporations.

They did things in a small way. Nobody really expected anything else.

Why? Why was Art Williams destined to be average and ordinary? Why was he supposed to settle for a modest standard of living and be satisfied with whatever life decided to dish out?

That's what I want to answer in this book. And I want to explain why Art Williams *did* make it, despite the whole world's view of what a success is supposed to look like.

I wrote this book because I got sick and tired of seeing people beaten down by society's messages.

I got sick and tired of seeing the kids I used to coach graduate with big hopes and big dreams, then get so put down in the world that they gave up before they had time to get started.

I got sick and tired of seeing people come to work at our company, wanting so bad to do something special with their lives but scared to death that they didn't have the right education or background or image.

You know, it's been twenty years since I first entered the business world as a part-time representative for a company that sold term insurance and investments. During that time I discovered some amazing things that I want to share with other people like me. I discovered that you don't have to have extraordinary abilities to succeed. You can be the most common person in the world and still do something uncommon with your life.

I figured out some secrets to winning, and I discovered some methods that worked for ordinary people like me, people whose only real credentials are a willingness to work and a burning desire to "be somebody." I want to share those secrets with those of you who are sitting out there, just like I was a short time ago, dying to do something special with your life and not knowing where to begin.

So many of the self-help books and motivational books leave me feeling empty. Many of them are written by people who experienced individual success in some area or who are great storytellers and motivational speakers. Other times, they're written by business "brains" who have developed some pretty elaborate theories about success.

It bothers me that even though many of these people have achieved personal success, a number of them have no track record of helping other people succeed. This group of people can tell their own unique story, but you have no real indication that their method of success will work in your life.

It's like diet books. Somebody goes out and loses weight and then writes a diet book. You can go to the bookstore and see hundreds of them. But most of the diets out there don't work. Government statistics show that only one out of every two hundred people who goes on a diet loses the weight he or she intended to lose and has kept it off a year later.

That can happen with self-help books, too. I believe that only a few of the people who read some of these new books get any real, long-range value out of them. Why? Because the methods in some of them haven't been proven on a mass scale; too often, they're nothing more than fancy phrases and pie-in-the-sky theory.

What's different about this book is that the principles set forth here have been proven; the system has been proven, not only in *my* life, but in the lives of literally *thousands* of other people. This system didn't work for just one person at one particular time and place; it has worked for many different people in many different situations, and it has stood the test of time.

Let me give you some examples.

✔ Rusty Crossland was a teacher and a coach making $10,000 a year when he came to work with A. L. Williams. He used the principles in this book, and today, Rusty has a million-dollar business, with revenues of $918,515 in 1987 alone.

✔ Lawrence Walker was a college student with no income at all when he got serious about winning. Last year he earned $291,082 and became a national sales director in our company.

✔ Brenda Sharp's business in Pasadena, California, earned her $206,135 in 1987, quite a jump from her former income of $23,000 a year as a home economist.

✔ Jerry Dancer was a lab technician in Phoenix, making $15,000 a year, when he started using these principles. Today, his business revenues are in six figures.

✔ Hubert Humphrey of Atlanta was a railroad engineer when he first heard about the success other people were having at our company. The $18,000 he was making on the railroad was considered a decent living at the time, but the $1,500,000 his business produced last year looks a lot better to him.

✔ Anne Baxter was a housewife who had never worked when family problems forced her to find a job. The principles in this book brought Anne her own business and a jump from no income to over $284,620 in less than five years.

These people, and hundreds more like them, will tell you that these principles work. And they'll work in *all areas* of your life. The principles in this book will help you build a championship football team, a championship business, or a championship family.

It doesn't matter if you're male or female, if you have a college education or no college education, if you're young or old. These fundamentals win in *life*.

Now, don't get me wrong. I'm not implying that success equals money. It's possible to be a champion in your business and personal life without having a lot of money. And it's possible to be a multimillionaire and still be a failure unless your success is built on a foundation of integrity, good character, and honest dealings with people. Success to me is achieving the goals and dreams that *you* have for your life, whatever those goals might be. It's becoming someone you can be proud of, making a difference with your life.

If you are like me, if you feel like you were put on this earth to do something special with your life, if you're always on fire, if you just can't stand being average and ordinary, if you want to "be somebody" so bad you can't stand it, even though everybody says you're not supposed to feel that way, this book is for you. Take its principles to heart and get ready to change your life in thirty days.

It's not pie in the sky. And I'm not saying it's easy. Changing your thinking and your actions never is. But I am saying it's worth it.

The title represents an underlying theme throughout this book. It's one of the biggest revelations I ever had on my path to becoming somebody special. It seems so simple, but it took me years to learn it (I guess that proves I'm not all that smart!). It's at the very heart of my program for winning. These nine words changed my life. They represent my realization that you don't have to be a genius to do something great with your life and become financially independent. You don't have to be the person in the magazine ads. You've got to be you, but you've got to be the very best you possibly can be. I realized that "all you can do is all you can do." But I also discovered that all you can do is *enough*.

The only reason I'm asking you to stick with me is that I've done it and I know this system works. And believe me, if it will work for somebody like me, it will work for you, too—regardless of your present circumstances.

Get started now. All you can do is all you can do, but all you can do—right now, where you are in your life this minute—is enough.

And . . . doing all you can do will change your life.

CHAPTER ONE

Everybody Wants to Be Somebody

A man is literally what he thinks.
James Allen

Everybody wants to be somebody. It's a fact of life. I believe the desire to be somebody is inherent in every living soul on this planet. No matter who we are or where we come from, deep down, all of us believe that we're special, we're different.

Everybody grows up with these kinds of feelings. When we're young, playing cowboys and Indians, everybody wants to be the sheriff. Kids watch TV, and they want to be an astronaut or a quarterback or a ballerina or a doctor. They watch the Olympics on TV, and they want to be skiers or figure skaters and win a gold medal. All kids are dreamers. It's as natural to them as breathing.

Recently, the teacher of a fifth-grade class here in Atlanta asked her students to write down their aspirations for future careers. Their answers will show you what I mean.

✔ The smallest boy in the class planned to be an Olympic gold medalist in swimming or luge!

✔ Two girls wanted to be president of the United States. (One was also considering being a lawyer or a judge.)

✔ One boy, who happened to be the 4-H talent show winner, couldn't decide between movie star and rock star. (My guess is that he'll be both!)

✔ A boy named Jason had the kind of ambition I love. In addition to being an F-14 pilot or a space explorer, he said he wanted to "be a quarterback for the Dallas Cowboys, and get M.V.P. *each season,* and make it to the Super Bowl *every year,* and *win!*"

There's nothing unusual about these kids. All kids play the "when I grow up" game. When they're young, it never occurs to them that there are any obstacles or barriers to their dreams. Their minds are filled with possibilities. They haven't had time to learn about responsibility. They haven't figured out yet that society is kindest to people who don't rock the boat. They haven't learned all the things you're *supposed* to say and think.

Their minds are free to dream the biggest dreams their hearts can produce. They don't know about obstacles; they just know about desire. They look down the road at their future and see one big open door leading to it.

And why not? All around them are positive sources of encouragement. They are protected in a cocoon, surrounded by parents and aunts and uncles and teachers telling them how special they are, how smart they are, how pretty they are, how wonderful they are. They feel like the center of the universe.

The Friday Night Feeling

I taught high school for seven years, and it was such a wonderful time. As a coach, I used to love Friday nights. The kids on the football team would be suiting up, and they'd be wired tight with the excitement of the game. The cheerleaders would be jumping up and down; the band would be playing the fight song; the fans would be screaming. Everybody was watching and rooting for us.

I think that's what I loved so much about coaching that age group. I loved seeing those kids full to the brim with all those big plans and big dreams in those years before they learned just how tough life can be.

At that time in their lives, the world was filled with excitement and new experiences. They were just starting to date, and their eyes were as big as baseballs. They were learning to drive and getting their licenses. They joined athletic teams or clubs or social groups. On the whole, they felt good about themselves and about their lives. Life was a bowl of cherries.

The Death of Dreaming

Everybody has that Friday night feeling as a young person.

What happens? What goes wrong once they become adults? Why are so many people disillusioned?

It's pretty simple, really.

They graduate from high school or college, and the big bad world slaps them in the face. They change jobs three or four times. Companies promise them everything and don't deliver anything. They get more and more frustrated. They get married and have a couple of kids. They get more responsibilities.

Then one day they wake up, roll out of bed, and think, *Life has passed me by. Life has dealt me a bad hand.* They are no longer vibrant, excited, pumped-up human beings. The people who once wanted to go out and conquer the world *have given up.*

Instead of feeling like they have choices and options in their lives, they develop an attitude of just taking it, just accepting whatever life seems to dish out. They start to accept being average and ordinary. They let life start running them.

I know exactly how the process works because I know how it worked in my life. I was the most fortunate guy in the world growing up because I had great parents. They were always so positive. My dad was a football coach, and he helped me and encouraged me all through my growing-up years.

When I got to high school, I had the greatest coaches in the world. Those two men, Tommy Taylor and West Thomas, helped me and boosted me up and made me feel like the most special person in the world. My little town of Cairo, Georgia, was unusual because, even though it had only ten thousand people, it had a commitment to young people like you wouldn't believe. The whole town supported the youth programs, and they provided the kids of Cairo with all the good experiences you can imagine.

I was one of those kids who grew up feeling like life was a beautiful experience. I went off to college and married my childhood sweetheart, Angela. Early on, I felt blessed.

Then I started experiencing a little of what the real world had to offer. My father died unexpectedly of a heart attack at age forty-eight. My mother had to struggle to make ends meet. It was hard for me to make a living. I fulfilled my dream of becoming a coach, but unfortunately, high-school coaches don't make much money, and I had a wife and two children to support.

I had a dream of financial security for my family, and I tried all kinds of things to earn extra money. But the great opportunities that I thought were out there just didn't materialize. I tried refereeing basketball games. I'd go out there on Friday night and run up and down the court for three hours and have all the parents and coaches screaming at me—for $12 a night.

One year, the coaches decided to sell Christmas trees. Imagine spending two weeks at night in the freezing cold handling those scratchy trees. When we divided up the money, we each got about $75 for our efforts.

Then I saw an ad in the newspaper that said, "Teachers and coaches, great part-time income." The job was selling encyclopedias. I was nervous about selling, but the commission was pretty good. I went away to a little training school and then started knocking on doors. I got more doors slammed in my face than I thought was possible! I was terrible at it. It got so every time I started toward a door, I got nauseated. My stomach went into knots. Finally, I sold two sets, one to my wife and one to a friend! Well, that experience was proof to me that I couldn't sell anything.

Still, I got excited when I went to a coaching clinic and met a guy who was just starting to market an exercise device. It was supposed to be the new wave of exercise machine for athletes. He promised me an exclusive franchise-type deal. I was really pumped up; I thought I was getting in on the ground floor of something big. I bought hundreds of the things, only to find out that everybody else in the South had been given the same kind of "franchise." Once again, I tried to put up with the rejection and that sick feeling every day. The bottom line was the same. The "device" didn't turn out to be a hit, and I ended up making $200 or $300 for all the rejection I took.

Sound familiar? Do you remember those experiences? I'll bet you do. We've all had them. Those are the kinds of experiences that dash your hopes and dreams right into the ground. You try your best, and you get so beat up that you don't even want to try anymore.

Even though I had experienced success selling insurance part-time, when I decided to form A. L. Williams I couldn't believe the put-downs I got. At every turn, I got beat up like you can't believe.

I remember when we were looking for a company to process the business we were selling. It was hard to get the heads of the insurance companies to talk to me. One time I had an appointment with a well-known company in Boston and felt pretty good after the meeting. Not long afterward, the president was in Atlanta, and he requested a meeting with me. I was so excited; I thought he was going to give me the news that they had decided to take our business. I met him downtown at the Peachtree Plaza Hotel to have dinner.

He looked me right in the eye and said, "Art, I have no doubt that you're going to fail."

He treated me badly, and it hurt. I just wanted to go home and crawl under the covers and not come out.

But I didn't. In the end, that man's reaction made me more determined than ever to win. I became determined not to be defeated by someone else's opinion of me or my ideas.

Is There Any Good News?

Folks, the good news is this: you don't have to take it. You don't have to continue your life this way. You don't have to just be average and ordinary. You don't have to let everybody put you down.

I believe we've got a problem in the United States. Over the last twenty-five years, the thinking in America has gotten mixed up. We've gotten off track. We've lost our belief in America as a land of opportunity where you can do whatever you want to do in life and be whatever you want to be. We'll talk more about our society's mixed-up thinking later on, but it's important to make that point here. Maybe you can't count on America as the land of opportunity anymore. But there's one thing you can still count on.

You can count on *you*.

If you want to win, here's the first step: you've got to start believing in you.

The Power of Believing

The first thing you've got to understand is the power of believing you're special, the power of believing you're different, the power of believing in your own abilities.

If you want to win, you've got to believe in yourself *again*.

✔ You've got to get back that childlike ability to dream— *again*.
✔ You've got to start believing you're special—*again*.
✔ You've got to see yourself winning—*again*.
✔ You've got to see yourself doing something special with your life, being somebody, being different—*again*.

I believe the *number-one problem* that keeps people from winning in the United States today is lack of belief in themselves. Once you grow up and let the world push you down, you lose the confidence you had when you were growing up. But you can get it back, and you must get it back if you want your life to change.

If you've got belief in yourself, you're richer than the Rockefellers. I remember a guy who showed up at one of our offices in Florida and wanted to work for A. L. Williams. He was about the most unimpressive guy you could ever meet. He drove up to the office in a truck—not a pickup truck, but a five-ton dump truck. He had on a plaid shirt and a different type of plaid shorts and bright red socks. Everybody sort of looked at this guy and said, "Whoa! What is this?"

All the managers in the group tried to pass him around. They were sure he didn't have a chance, so nobody wanted to waste valuable time with him. Well, he kept coming back. Finally, the regional vice president (RVP) at the office gave in and hired him. When the new recruit was getting started, the RVP reluctantly climbed up into the dump truck and went on appointments with him.

Today, the man in the dump truck is a regional vice president himself, earning around $10,000 *a month*. Society says that this guy didn't have a chance. He didn't look right; he didn't drive the right car.

But this guy *believed* he could do the business. He believed he had a chance to change his life, to do something different, something more challenging, and succeed. It really didn't matter to him what anybody thought. He believed he could do it, and he refused to be discouraged by any of the negative feelings he encountered.

This man had the power of belief in himself. And it paid off. (P.S. Jerry Clingenpeel still wears red socks—and today, *nobody* is laughing.)

You might say, "Art, that's not how it is in the real world. When you get to be an adult, you've got to accept things the way they are. People like me can't win."

Ridiculous!

You don't have to accept a thing. OK? That's loser talk. That's the way losers think. That's why people are losing out there, because they accept things. Life will give you what you'll fight for.

Jerry Dancer wasn't a "natural" athlete. Yet, after years and years of hard work, he was named Athlete of the Year in his small Texas town. Several major colleges scouted his games and expressed interest in signing him to a full scholarship. His goals were to go to college, play baseball, and study to be a dentist.

At that time in his life, like most people, Jerry was on top of the world.

Then the "real world" hit him in the face. He wasn't quite good enough to get a full athletic scholarship. In the end, the offers were for partial scholarships, and his family couldn't afford the rest. He had difficulty with his classes and dropped out of college. He returned to his hometown to work with his dad at the chemical company.

One day Jerry looked up and felt like his life was over. He didn't have a college degree. He wasn't a baseball player. He wasn't a dentist. In his mind, he was a nobody.

Jerry had given up. He had stopped trying, stopped competing. One day, he met someone from our company who thought he would be great in our business. But Jerry wasn't interested. He looked at the company a few times, but he turned it down. He just didn't believe anything good could still happen.

After nine months of saying no, Jerry felt a little stirring of belief deep inside. Maybe—just maybe—he could do it. Maybe there was a chance. He finally decided to go for it. He turned his life around. Today, Jerry's a national sales director, one of our highest management positions. He supervises a large organization and enjoys a lifestyle he never imagined back at the chemical company. He can look back and see how close he came to giving up on his life and accepting less than life has to offer.

You know, everybody wants to end up like Jerry Dancer. Everybody would love to be successful. Everybody would love to be financially independent, love to have a successful business. But that just isn't good enough. You've got to show up and fight for it.

Get Ready to Fight for What You Want

So many people feel like their lives belong to somebody else. They feel like they've lost control, like they are puppets and somebody else is pulling the strings.

Wrong! Right now—this minute—you must abandon that belief if you want to succeed.

UNWRITTEN LAW: *Life will give you whatever you'll accept.*

✔ If you'll accept being average and ordinary, life will make you average and ordinary.
✔ If you'll accept being unhappy, life will make you unhappy.
✔ If you'll accept having financial problems, that's what life will give you.

But if you won't accept those things, in most areas of life you can have anything you want. If you demand happiness, success, and fulfillment, that's exactly what you'll get.

There's another unwritten law:

UNWRITTEN LAW: *Life will turn out the way you see it turning out.*

That's reality. People have been so put upon, they see failure and disappointment and unhappiness. That's exactly how life's going to turn out for you if that's what you see.

You've got to start seeing happiness and success and fulfillment in your life.

If you take the position that your life just hasn't worked out, you just didn't get the breaks, you've given up. The next step is to sit down and quit.

That's where most people are in America today.

If you're at the stage right now where you've had two or three companies let you down, you're frustrated and unhappy, you feel like a total failure . . . there's still hope for you.

If you want to do it badly enough, you can still change and become everything you wanted to become when you were a youngster.

To do that, you've got to get these *power principles* into your brain.

Power Principle #1: *You've got to demand for yourself happiness and success.*

The world isn't going to give you anything. Nobody's going to come along, tap you on the shoulder, and hand you an opportunity. People will tap you on the shoulder and maybe knock the daylights out of you when you turn around. That's about all you'll get for free.

Most people already know that. But they think that since nobody's going to help them, they don't have a chance.

Wrong again!

Nobody's going to walk up and hand you a great opportunity, but guess what? You don't need anybody else because you've got the power to be successful *inside you*. All you need is the belief that you deserve a place in this world and the determination to get it. You've got to demand that for yourself.

A young boy in a west Tennessee town had a tough life with none of the advantages his schoolmates had. He wasn't even allowed to visit his best friend, Jimmy, because Jimmy's parents claimed that the boy was from the wrong side of the tracks. Some folks called him "white trash." But the boy had the desire to do something special.

He had a guitar, but he didn't know how to tune it. When Jimmy's cousin, country star Lonzo Green, came to visit, the boy took his battered, secondhand guitar and met the singer in a lane near the house. Feeling sorry for the boy, the singer showed him how to tune the instrument and took the time to show him a few basic chords. It wasn't much, but the boy from the wrong side of the tracks didn't expect much. All he needed was an opportunity, a chance.

Just a few short years later, the boy who was believed to be "not good enough" by Jimmy's parents won the hearts of Americans everywhere. As a young man, Elvis Presley took what little help he found, turned it into opportunity, and demanded for himself a place in the world.

Power Principle #2: *You've got to learn to dream again.*

Stop telling yourself what you *can't* do. Start thinking about what you really want from life. Let your mind open up to the possibilities like you did in high school. Retrieve those old dreams and dust them off. Practice dreaming every day. You can feel like you did before if you let your imagination go free.

Believe in yourself. Two-thirds of the battle is in your mind. Henry Ford said, "Whether you think you can or think you can't—you're right." It's true, folks. Belief in yourself is *power.*

Rickey Allman was making a comfortable living in 1979. He had a job as a truck driver, earning between $25,000 and $30,000 a year, and he owned several rental apartments. Then, the bottom fell out. Rickey injured his knee at work. He needed several expensive operations. The bank foreclosed on the apartments, and Rickey lost everything. When he came to work with A. L. Williams, he was $750,000 in debt.

How could a guy who had experienced this kind of disappointment ever dream again? What was left but giving up?

But Rickey Allman did dream again. And he held onto his dream through the toughest times. When Rickey joined our company, he had nothing. His first three years in the business, he barely covered expenses. Almost everybody told him to give up. But he hung on to his dream of financial revival for his family. In 1987, Rickey became a member of our $100,000 club, and he hopes to become a senior vice president soon. He and his family are making great progress toward wiping away all their debt and meeting their goal of financial security.

Power Principle #3: *You've got to compete.*

In addition to dreaming, young people get out there and fight. They're on either high-school teams or Little League teams, and they're out there competing. They want to be somebody. They're not going to give up. They're going to fight.

The last time most people really competed was in high school or college. In the adult world, you've got to hang on to that good feeling about yourself, you've got to see yourself winning, and you've got to get out there and compete. You've got to go to work. Man, you've got to put on your boxing gloves and go out there and fight.

We've all heard this story before, but it says more about the ability to keep competing than anything else I've ever heard. Our nation's greatest leader knew defeat throughout his life. He lost eight elections, failed in business twice, and suffered a nervous breakdown. His path to success looked like this:

1831—Failed in business.
1832—Defeated for legislature.
1833—Second failure in business.
1836—Suffered nervous breakdown.
1838—Defeated for speaker.
1840—Defeated for elector.
1843—Defeated for Congress.
1848—Defeated for Congress.
1855—Defeated for Senate.
1856—Defeated for vice president.
1858—Defeated for Senate.
1860—ELECTED PRESIDENT OF THE UNITED STATES.

Abraham Lincoln was a champion who never stopped competing, even with a pattern of failure that would have left most of us devastated. He just kept competing—until he won.

Power Principle #4: *You can change.*

It's not too late to change. Wherever you are in your life, there's still time to jump back into the game, to ask more from life than you've been asking in the past.

Will Kellogg was forty-six before he made the decision to go into business for himself. He was a shy man with few friends, limited interests, and no discernible talents. Until that time, he worked for his older brother, a prominent yet stingy doctor who never paid Will more than $87 a month.

While experimenting with producing cereal for some of

Dr. Kellogg's patients, the two men discovered the wheat flake. Will tried to convince his brother to mass-market the flake, but Dr. Kellogg refused. In 1906, Will finally stepped out of the shadow, buying his brother's share of their cereal-making patents and forming his own cereal company.

Given the chance to be his own boss, the once shy, ordinary man exhibited a business genius that few would have believed he possessed. Will became one of the first advertisers to use color magazine ads, test markets, and widespread sampling. His first product was corn flakes.

The rest is history. In a short time, Will Kellogg became one of the nation's richest men.

Will Kellogg looked like he was a beaten man. But he had a power that his brother didn't have—he believed in himself. Even though his life had been far from exciting and success seemed a long way off, Will hadn't stopped dreaming. He hadn't completely lost that Friday night feeling. He still wanted to be somebody.

It's not too late for you to be somebody, either. There's still time. You *can* do it.

All you have to do is *recognize the power of believing in yourself and your God-given potential.* You know what will happen? As you'll see in the next chapter, everybody else probably won't believe in you. Society probably won't. Your friends and relatives probably won't. Your spouse may not even believe in you.

But you know what? If *you* believe, none of that will matter.

CHAPTER TWO

Warning: Failure Messages Ahead

Always bear in mind that your own resolution to succeed is more important than any other one thing.
Abraham Lincoln

Did you ever wonder why people lose the dreams of their childhood, dreams like becoming famous or living in a fine home or owning their own business or making a lot of money? I don't think it happens by chance. I've found there's a definite reason that people seem to just self-destruct.

Let me give you an example of what happened to me. My dad was a coach, and as a youngster, all I thought about doing was coaching football. I married a girl I fell in love with in the second grade, the only real girlfriend I ever had. We got married my freshman year in college and had both our children before we graduated.

Two years after we graduated, I got my first head football coaching job at the high-school level and was very successful. Two years after that, I became head football coach and athletic director at a great high school in the biggest league in Georgia. And I was named Coach of the Year two out of my five years as a head coach. It seemed I was really going to the top in a hurry. My life was a dream come true. My wife was a schoolteacher. We weren't making much money, but we were happy. We had a comfortable living, and I had my master's degree from Auburn University thinking that, like most coaches, somewhere down the road I could become a principal. It was everything I had dreamed it would be.

And yet, I was frustrated. Art Williams was a little disappointed. I wanted more out of life than just being comfortable. I wanted to "be somebody." I wanted to make a difference. So when I found a company that sold a different concept about life insurance and investments, I was so excited. I said to myself, "Man, this is it! My opportunity! My chance to really be somebody!" When I went home to tell my wife, I said, "Angela! I want to sell life insurance."

Angela was shocked and worried. She looked at me, and she said, "Art, our life is so great. People like you. They respect you. We have a nice house. We have a wonderful family. We're saving a little money. Everything's so good. Why do you want to give that up and throw all our dreams out the window?"

I was getting what I call a "failure message" from Angela. For the first six months I was in the business, Angela wouldn't even tell her parents what I was doing. "He's in investments," she'd say under her breath.

Failure messages . . . the hardest ones to take come from your family and friends. And that's what people experience throughout life—negative messages about their dreams that just devastate them.

Negatives on Every Front

Think about the world we live in. It's impossible to get away from failure messages. Americans today are bombarded with negatives, the kind of negatives that make them abandon their dreams and give up.

A major problem lies with television news. Twenty years ago, you had a fifteen-minute national newscast. Then a few years later, that went to thirty minutes. Then the local people had to have a thirty-minute news show before the national news. Then they expanded that to an hour. And now a television network gives twenty-four-hour news.

Do you know what that does to the American public? It

hits us with 99 percent negatives. Now, not only do we have to worry about our own problems and our own families, which is enough to destroy most people, but we've got to worry about the problems of the whole world. And it hits us every day. We watch TV, and we worry about

- ✔ *Nuclear war.* People say we're living in an age where we'll probably have a nuclear war. So why try? Why try to save money and be somebody? It's not going to matter because the whole world's going to blow up!
- ✔ *Record federal deficits.* We're facing the largest budget deficit in our history, and it's getting larger every day. The message is, well, why work?
- ✔ *Trade imbalance.* America has lost its lead in the world. Now we're having to take a backseat to Germany and Japan and other countries. We're going to lower our standard of living because we're not as productive as we used to be. The message? Just give up.
- ✔ *The stock market.* In October 1987, we experienced one of the worst stock market declines in the history of our country. Don't take any risks.
- ✔ *Lost morality.* Some of the presidential candidates have shown no morals or scruples. They're having affairs with women and admitting to plagiarism. Evangelists who minister to millions and millions of people are being exposed as nothing but hypocrites. Is there anyone we can trust?
- ✔ *Crime.* Rape and murder are hot television show topics. The world's a fearful place to live in.

The average person watches hours of TV every day, and that's the kind of garbage filling the viewer's mind.

As if that wasn't enough, there's another set of failure messages that we have to wrestle with. I believe that people who look like you and me have to fight against a conspiracy that is out to program America. I believe that the big universities started it. Then the big corporations and, ultimately, our whole society have tried to program people to think that if you are born rich and born on the "right side of the tracks," you are privileged, you go to college, and you get the good jobs. But if you are born poor or come from an average background, you must give up your big dreams and ambitions. Or if you have a high IQ, you are brilliant, and you deserve the best jobs. But if you have an average or a low IQ, you must take the low-level, low-paying jobs.

Dead wrong.

Most companies have committees that judge applicants only by college degrees, college board scores, experience, background, references, recommendations, and so on.

Dumb. Dumb. Dumb.

Companies put too much emphasis on resumes. If you've ever failed in business before, they brand you a loser.

Ridiculous!

Testing has become a fact of life in American business. People are judged by how high they score on aptitude tests, personality tests, and achievement tests.

Wrong again.

I have a perfect example of how wrong this is and how damaging it can be. A friend from a small town in Alabama told me a story about his brother. When his brother was in high school, he was well liked by his fellow students, but he just didn't test well. And it wasn't because he didn't work hard; the light would be on in his room until late at night as he studied for each test. One of his best friends, however, always did exceptionally well in class.

When they were juniors, the two boys took the college entrance exams together. The "smart" one did pretty well, but the other boy made a terrible score. He made the mistake of telling his friend. As a cruel joke, whenever his friend would see him across the school campus, he'd call out his score as if he were calling his name, "Hey, 680!" Of course, the other boys would laugh at the joke, and the poor boy would try to laugh, too. But it was humiliating, and he just wanted to die inside.

Today, the two boys are grown, and you know what? The

boy who didn't test well is making $75,000 a year in the real estate business and is approaching financial independence. The "smart" boy was penniless before the age of thirty and still can't hold a job.

There never has been and there never will be a test that can look inside a person and tell if he has what it takes. No one can accurately judge a person by looking at his background. College degrees and IQs aren't the secret. The key to winning in business is what's inside a person. Character and people abilities are the most important abilities. Common sense is far more important than book sense. But you'll never catch an English professor saying that!

I've received failure messages all my life. One day, when I was coaching, I read an ad in the newspaper: "Executive search. Call this number." I figured, Why not? I had a college degree. Maybe I ought to talk to them and give it a shot. So I set up an appointment and drove all the way to Atlanta. I got on the elevator and went up sixteen floors in a big building. They sat me down and gave me all these aptitude tests, and then I left and never heard from them again. Never even called me back to tell me whether I'd passed or failed. Didn't even bother. All they saw was a football coach with a physical education degree. How do you think that made me feel? It was like a slap in the face.

All of a sudden there was something inside me saying, "Art, you dummy. Who do you think you are? You're not meant to run a company. You can't compete with those guys in their pin-striped suits." But you know what? I made a choice. The most important choice, I believe, of my career. I chose not to listen to that failure message.

You see, I believe there are two kinds of Americas. One is led by the doom-and-gloom crowd who let other people influence them. The other America is led by people who choose to look at life as a challenge. That's the America I chose.

It's Your Choice

Folks, failure messages will hit you from every direction. They come from society, your family, your friends, and they all say the same thing: "You can't." "Impossible." "Not for the average Jane or Joe." "Not for somebody who looks like you."

But the beauty of America is that you've got a choice. You can ignore them.

FAILURE MESSAGE	MY CHOICE
Not "smart"	Common sense
Not "pretty"	Character will win
Not athletic	Trains harder
Give up	Never quit
Life's not fair	Accepts responsibility for success *and* failure
Bad times coming	Best time to succeed/ positive attitude

You can give in to the failure messages and be a bitter deadbeat full of excuses. Or you can choose to be happy and positive and excited about life.

When I coached at Kendrick High School in Columbus, Georgia, a black student came up to me one day. His name was Rudy Allen. He was a little ol' bitty thing in the eighth grade. He played in the band. He said, "Coach, I want to play football, and I want to be the first black quarterback at this high school." Now you talk about handicaps. This boy was at a high school in Georgia. He was skinny, not the athletic type. But he had a dream. He'd get out there and throw the football and work out, long after all the other kids had gone home to watch TV. His junior year, Rudy led us to the championship, and two years later, he received a full athletic scholarship to Georgia Tech, so he played quarterback there, too.

Now, folks, do you think Rudy heard the failure messages? If anyone ever heard them, *he* did. But Rudy made a choice. He could have taken the easy way and played in the band until he was a senior and still have been skinny and then graduated, and to this day he would have wondered what it would have been like to play football at a major university.

Is that where you are in your life? Still wondering what if . . . ?

Do you think it's too late? I read recently in a weekly news magazine that a record number of millionaires were created last year. Think about it. In spite of all our faults and all our problems, in spite of all our deficits, all the rapes, murders, and terrorism, more people became financially successful last year than in any other year in the history of our country.

You could be one of those people. But you've got to get excited about life. And when your family and friends look at you and say, "You? Do that? Just go back to your room," or they just roll their eyes and say, "Well, that's the tenth time I've heard that," that's when you've got to have the courage of a Rudy Allen and see those failure messages for what they are.

Conquer the Next Mountain

I believe that this is the perfect time for you to make a decision to change your life. Our country has become so soft that it's that much easier for the really tough people to make it.

Think about the hardships our forefathers went through. They came to this country with the same dreams that you and I have, to control their own destiny and find a greater opportunity for their families. But really think about the incredible *physical* conditions they endured—weeks and weeks over the ocean in a wooden ship that leaked. When they arrived, they literally had nothing. They had to build settlements with crude tools, and even after they were settled, they faced terrible illness with almost no medical attention. The amazing thing is, they went through all that heartache for *exactly the same things* that you and I want: an opportunity to be somebody and to control our own destiny. Just *imagine* the little problems every day that we let defeat us. I believe that the masses of people in this country have stopped trying. They've given up and let failure messages rule their lives.

The key? *You* don't have to be that way. You can take advantage of the dream of opportunity that this country was built on.

You know, despite the fact that I've already reached financial independence, I still want to go out there and conquer the next mountain. When they click my lights out for the last time, I want people to be able to say, "Man, That guy was a stud, that guy was *somebody.*"

Failure messages will hit you from every direction. You've got to be tough and ready for them.

Everyone talks these days about the big leagues. The National Football League is not the big leagues. The National Basketball Association is not the big leagues. The major leagues in baseball are not the big leagues. You know what the "big leagues" is? It's your life. It doesn't get any bigger than your life. And you have only one. You're here for just a flicker. It's unbelievable how short life really is.

What's going to happen with yours? Will you listen to the failure messages and let them destroy your hope? Which America will you choose: the gloom-and-doom America or the America that sees this country as a land of opportunity? I hope that, like Rudy and me, you choose the latter.

CHAPTER THREE

The Secret to Winning

Nothing stops the man who desires to achieve. Every obstacle is simply a course to develop his achievement muscle. It's a strengthening of his powers of accomplishment.

Eric Butterworth

Y ou've discovered why you stopped dreaming, and you're on your way to believing in yourself. You know what the secret to winning is *not*. It's not talent, it's not looks, it's not a college degree or a privileged background.

So what is it?

I can explain it to you in just one word.

Are you ready?

The secret to winning is *desire*.

Sometimes I call it "want to." Sometimes I call it "will to win." No matter what you call it, it's the secret that most people overlook because they're so busy worrying about the things they think they don't have.

Josif Brifman was one of the elite in Russian society. He was a big executive, responsible for building the largest computer company in the Soviet Union. But Josif and his wife, Dina, became more and more unhappy with Soviet life. Josif was Jewish, and Jews were held in low esteem. Josif had pretty much stayed out of politics, but as his position in Russian society increased, he came to feel that the Soviet leadership and bureaucracy amounted to little more than a large-scale Mafia organization.

In 1979, Josif and Dina took advantage of agreements made with the Soviet Union during the Carter administration, plus the help of some high-placed friends, and managed to get to Vienna. From there they came to the United States, with big dreams of owning a business of their own. They settled in Dallas, Texas.

Things began to work out for Josif; he got a job immediately because of his computer expertise, even though he couldn't speak English. Still, the idea of being "managed" by someone else didn't fit with Josif's dream of freedom and opportunity. Josif's desire kept burning inside him. He kept looking for that opportunity to "do something special."

While Josif was trying to buy a house, his realtor told him about our company and invited him to take a look at it. At first he had reservations. Insurance in Russia was handled by the state, and private insurance companies didn't exist. He didn't know anything about insurance, and the language problem was a gigantic barrier to a sales career.

But Josif saw one thing that started him thinking—the opportunity to be his own boss, run his own business with no limits on his income. He could earn just as much as he could make; it was all up to him. That was what he and Dina had been looking for.

Now, think about it. Here's a guy who speaks very little English, knows nothing about the lifestyle of Americans (which was very different from his own), doesn't know anything about sales, doesn't know a soul in town, has no natural market of friends, relatives, or acquaintances. And he's going to go out and make a living as a life insurance representative. Ridiculous, right?

Wrong.

It would be ridiculous if you didn't count Josif's desire. Yes, a lot of people shook their heads. Even some of his managers felt sorry for him; they didn't think he had a chance. But Josif didn't see it that way. When a manager told him he should try to make ten sales call a day, Josif decided to make seventy calls. He knew it was going to take an extra effort. Since he didn't know anyone, he just started knocking on doors. For four months, he didn't make one sale. Not one! He had one rejection after another. But he hung on. He knew this was a chance, and he had to make it work or go back to working for somebody else.

The first two years in the business, Josif barely made ends meet. But in 1984, Josif's hard work and endurance paid off. His earnings jumped dramatically. In 1986, he was promoted to the senior vice president level. Josif became an inspiration among people in the company. If he could make it with all the obstacles he faced, anybody could make it. A lot of people looked at Josif, quit complaining about how hard their job was, and went to work.

Desire. It's more powerful than any other ingredient in the winning formula. Some people want to win so bad that they can't stand it. They get up every morning and go to bed every night dreaming about winning. Even though their head tells them they can't, something deep inside tells them that they've got to.

I don't know why I'm like I am. I want to be somebody, amount to something. I want my wife and kids to look at me and be proud. I just can't live with being average and ordinary.

One of the most sensational boxing matches of this century was held between Sugar Ray Leonard and Marvin Hagler. Leonard challenged Hagler for the middleweight championship. But there were some problems. Sugar Ray had retired from boxing because of a detached retina in his eye. He had been warned by his doctors that a blow to his eye could cause total blindness. It was crazy for Sugar Ray to consider getting back into the ring. He was an Olympic champion, world professional champion, wealthy—he had everything. He hadn't been training, he wasn't even close to being in the same condition as the fierce Hagler, and he couldn't afford to take a chance on a hit to the eye.

But nobody understood Leonard's desire. He was a winner, a champion. He had to prove that he was the greatest middleweight to ever get inside the ropes. He just wanted it so bad. Leonard went back into training with a vengeance. On the

night of the fight, the world watched as Leonard beat Hagler—
not by a knockout, but by being tougher and lasting longer—to
regain his title of Middleweight Champion of the World.

Now, stop for a minute. Just think about it. Folks, desire
isn't almost everything; it *is* everything. Another great athlete,
Earvin "Magic" Johnson, summed it up like this: "Even when I
went to the playground, I never picked the best players. I picked
the guys with less talent, but those who were willing to work
hard and had the *desire* to be great."

If others tell you that the secret to winning is anything else,
they're only misleading you.

✔   If you have a good education, great! But you won't win
    without desire.
✔   If you have talent, great! But talent won't help if you
    don't have desire.
✔   Did you say you were good looking? Super! But you'll
    still fail if you don't have the desire.
✔   So you don't have talent or a great education? Great!
    With desire, you can still win.
✔   And you aren't very good looking? Terrific! If you have
    desire, you can win in spite of everything.

Desire is the secret. You can have everything else in the
world going for you, and if you don't have the desire to be
somebody, if you don't want to go out there and change your
own destiny, there's no hope for you. But if you do, if you want
it enough, no obstacle can stop you.

Have I made it perfectly clear? *Desire is the key.* If you've got
desire, you can be anything you want to be in America today,
provided you have two things: a specific goal and a plan.

This isn't a trick. Desire *is* everything, but these two things
are essential to give your desire the direction it must have to
make things happen.

The Most Revolutionary Lesson of My Life

When I was just getting started selling term life insurance
part-time, something happened that changed my life. At that

time, I had discovered term insurance and had become a crusader for the cause. I had always had a burning desire to become successful, but now, finally, my newfound crusade had given me a cause worth fighting for. I was ready to "do it," but I didn't know how to begin.

Then something revolutionary happened. I went to a sales seminar, and the speaker said, "If you haven't read *Think and Grow Rich*, run to the nearest bookstore and get a copy." I was looking for any kind of help, so I went straight to the bookstore after the seminar ended.

I'm a slow reader, so I only made it to page 36. But what I found on that page of Napoleon Hill's *Think and Grow Rich* literally changed my life. Now, I don't agree with Hill's opinions and beliefs in a lot of areas, but his advice on success is powerful.

Hill spent a lifetime studying successful people, looking for the "common denominator" that they all shared. He found that *every* successful person he studied—not every other person— did these two things: set a specific goal and devised a plan for achieving that goal.

Hill came up with his own six-step plan. I followed the plan, and I stuck to it. And you know what? It worked. I'm not just kidding around here. I believe that these six steps led me to success. I had always had the desire, but Hill's plan defined the desire that I had been looking for all my life.

I'm modifying Hill's words here to show you specifically how the plan worked in my life, but these are the basic steps.

Step #1: *You must have a specific goal.*

At the time, I was making $10,700 a year as athletic director and head football coach at Kendrick High School in Georgia. I agonized for days, and I decided that, for me, one of the most important things was financial independence for my family. I figured that meant enough money to have an income of $30,000 a year for life. (Today, that doesn't sound very ambitious, but it seemed like a fortune to me at the time.) If I accumulated $300,000 cash and got 10 percent interest, I could withdraw $30,000 each year forever without touching the principal.

Step #2: *You must have a specific time in which to achieve your goal.*

I was twenty-eight, so I gave myself ten years. I would be financially independent by my thirty-eighth birthday. I committed to whatever work and sacrifice were necessary for ten years.

Step #3: *You must write down your goal.*

Everything seems more important if it's in writing. When you make your commitment to a specific goal, write it down and put it where you'll see it often. (I wrote mine down on a piece of cardboard and put it on my daily calendar.)

Step #4: *You must develop a plan to achieve your goal.*

I had been selling insurance part-time for two and a half years. I had saved all the money I made at that and had $42,000 in my savings account. If I could get a 10 percent return on my savings, that would come to over $100,000 in ten years. (I rounded it off to $100,000 to keep it simple.)

That was great, but I was still $200,000 short of my goal!

At 10 percent interest, I would have to save roughly $1,000 a month for ten years to get the extra $200,000.

I had my plan. I'd invest my $42,000 for ten years and invest $1,000 a month for ten years, and I'd have the $300,000 that would give me $30,000 a year for life.

Step #5: *You must decide the price you are willing to pay.*

Saving $1,000 a month from commission income was going to be tough. But nobody said financial independence was easy. It was all a matter of how important my dream of financial freedom was to me.

I knew I couldn't do it on my coaching salary. I would have a better chance if I went full-time into the insurance business. I believed in what I was doing, but I loved coaching, too. Yet there was no way I could achieve my goal and stay in coaching.

My price would be to give up coaching. That was the toughest decision of my life, tougher than anything that came later. I had grown up wanting to be a coach and training to be one. I had been very successful. It was a great job. But my dreams for me and my family came first, and I burned my bridges to make a new start at my dreams.

Step #6: *You must think about reaching your goal every day.*

Not one day went by that I didn't dream and think about the goal I had set. Thinking about how great it would be to be totally financially independent kept me going a million times when I wanted to quit. A well-known quote says, "Obstacles are those frightful things you see when you take your eyes off your goals," and it's true. My dreams kept me going, but my goals kept me on course.

I'm telling you, folks, don't pass over this section lightly. We're talking here about something that can help you change your life. I know these six steps work. If you're serious about doing something special with your life, sit down *today* and get started with the six steps for yourself. You can't do it overnight. It might take days or weeks, but how bad do you want to be somebody?

The Four Principles of Desire

Desire has a power all its own. It's not just a fluke. Desire is such a powerful force because once you act on your desire, a pattern develops that will take you a long way down the road to success.

Principle #1: *Desire gains strength when it has a concrete form.*

Napoleon Hill recognized an important truth. Goal setting

is the key to focusing your desire into a workable form. There's no mystery to it. Goal setting does three very important things:

First, *goal setting forces you to decide exactly what your dream is.* A lot of people dream about becoming rich or being famous. Those dreams are OK, but they're so vague you can't get a handle on them. Forcing yourself to set goals makes you take a hard look at what you really want from life.

Second, *goals turn "want to" into "to do."* No football coach would dream of going into the locker room before a game and just saying, "Go get 'em, guys." You've got to have a specific game plan. Once you decide what you want and work out a reasonable strategy for achieving it, you'll know exactly what to do when you get up each day.

Third, *having a goal helps you measure your progress.* In other words, it keeps you from cheating. It's one thing to say, "Today I'm going to improve." There's no real way to measure that at the end of the day. It allows you to slide a little without feeling too badly. But if your goal is to talk to four prospective new clients today, you have a clear way to measure your success—or failure. Psychologically, it makes all the difference.

Principle #2: *Desire becomes obsession.*

Once you've set your specific goal, you've got to keep it in front of you all the time. You've got to make it an *obsession.* Write it down. Read it every day. Think about it until it becomes as much a part of you as breathing.

Look at the young athletes who have an Olympic gold medal as their long-term goal in life. Did you ever stop to think what they go through to achieve that goal? When the rest of their friends are playing, they go to the practice rink or field. Often they practice early in the morning, before school, and late into the evening. Weekends and holidays are simply chances to squeeze in more practice time. In many ways, they experience childhood and young adulthood from the sidelines.

What drives these young people to make these sacrifices? They start with a dream, turn that dream into a goal, and eventually that goal, pursued with intensity, becomes an obsession. They eat, sleep, and breathe their goal, nearly twenty-four hours a day. Theirs is a relentless effort to turn their goal into a reality.

My friend Chip Taylor, a senior vice president in St. Louis, understands that level of intensity. A friend told me a story about Chip when he was first starting out that made a real impression on me. Chip really believed in our company; he was a crusader from the word *go*. One day he was between appointments and left the office to run down the hall to the rest room. He was gone a long time, and his manager began to wonder about him. He stuck his head out the office door and heard Chip talking.

The manager saw Chip at the corner near the soft drink machine. The soft drink man was standing there filling the machine. He had the door wide open and a big sack of money there beside him as Chip talked to him about the company. All of a sudden, Chip started to walk back to the office, bringing the soft drink man with him. The man was so excited that he had walked off and left the drink machine wide open and the bag of money sitting there on the floor. And Chip still hadn't made it to the men's room.

That's the kind of attitude that builds winners. Chip was obsessed with what he was doing, just like the Olympic athletes. He had a burning desire to tell everyone he saw about what he was doing. Today, Chip is a winner beyond his wildest dreams. He's reached "gold medal" territory within our company, and he did it because he became obsessed with achieving the goals he had set for himself.

Principle #3: *Desire becomes a commitment.*

Once you've rooted your desire so firmly in your mind that you think about it all the time, your desire becomes a commitment. You're ready to go beyond thinking and dreaming and really commit to devoting your time and energy to obtaining your desire.

When you make a commitment, you've got to burn all your bridges. There's a famous story about a general who literally burned his bridges. He had taken his army by boat to meet the enemy, who dramatically outnumbered his own forces. When everyone had gotten off the boats, the general ordered the boats burned. As their only source of escape went up in flames, the general told his men that since they couldn't escape, they must either win the battle or die. The army won.

On the spot, those soldiers made a commitment to win. It will work the same way in your life. Once you make a commitment, you gain that little extra ounce of courage to keep you going when things get tough.

In all my years in business, I've seen a definite pattern in the way commitment works. It's not instant. You don't develop it immediately. Even when you think you have it, you usually don't. I've observed that nearly all people go through three stages before they reach the level of commitment that will see them through the disappointments and heartaches.

THE LYING STAGE

Deep down, you aren't sure you can do it. But you can't admit that to anyone, not even yourself. For the first few months, you lie to everybody you know. You just lie and lie and lie. You act excited and pumped up about some opportunity, some idea, or some turn of events that encourages you and makes you walk three feet off the floor. You tell your spouse, "Honey, I always knew you married a winner. Just get ready, we're going to the top now. I've found my thing. I've found my place in life." You tell your mom and dad and all your relatives how you're going to make them proud of you. You tell your friends to watch your smoke. You are really getting ready to do something great.

But then it happens. You go home at night, and you go into the bathroom and close the door. You walk across the room and look in the mirror. "Bam!" It hits you right across the face like a cold rag. You look at that person in the mirror, and you say to yourself, "Who are you kidding? Do you think somebody who looks like you is going to make it? What have you ever done in your life? Why don't you just admit that nobody as ordinary as you can be a big success?"

Then you crawl in bed, and you want to go to sleep so bad you can't stand it. Your spouse is over there snoring, and your eyes are as big as baseballs. You want to make it so bad you're just burning up inside. You stare at the ceiling and hope you can survive one more week.

But you can't hope your way to the top.

THE QUITTING STAGE

Once you're through the lying stage, you enter the second stage—the quitting stage. You've gone out there and paid a fantastic price for two, three, maybe five months. Then you lose a client, or you hear a string of "noes." You start saying, "I've had it. I'm sick and tired of this. I'm going to go out and get a good job." You go out for two or three days and look around, maybe go to a few interviews. Then the realization hits you. There aren't any good jobs for people who want to be somebody.

So you say to yourself, "Well, I thought I was working hard. I thought I was committed. But I wasn't. I'm never going to see myself this low again. I'll do it this time, no matter what!" You go out there and work even harder for a few months, then you can't find a good prospect or one of your plans blows up in your face. You say, "I'm sick of this. I'm going to get a good job and quit beating my head against a wall."

But once again you find out that the great opportunity you want just doesn't exist out there in the corporate world. So you say, "I guess there aren't any good jobs in this country for people who look like me. I'm so sick of feeling like this and having financial problems and seeing other people get ahead, I can't stand it. Right now, I'm going to start all over. I'll work three times as hard. You're looking at one dude who's going to the top."

THE "DO IT" STAGE

All of a sudden, you get through the quitting stage. You make that final commitment, the one that really counts. Now you're on the road to greatness. Don't expect to recognize when you've finally entered the real commitment stage. You probably won't realize that you've made the final commitment for sixty or ninety days, when the results of your commitment start to show.

This may sound silly to you, but I promise you it's going to happen. The three stages are as real as rain. Recognize the lying stage and the quitting stage as normal.

The message about all this is that it's tough to make a total commitment. It's not an overnight decision; it's a long, ongoing process.

When I was speaking in Florida, I had a conversation with one of our senior vice presidents. He told me that six years ago he was $150,000 in debt. His life was going down the tubes. He told me that his family and friends advised him to declare bankruptcy, move out of the state, and start a new life. But the guy wouldn't do it. He had the kind of desire and commitment that made him say, "I don't care how bad the problems are, I'm not going to let anybody make me quit. I'm supposed to amount to something." The man didn't declare bankruptcy, and he slowly worked his way out of his debts.

He didn't have to tell me he was going to make it. I could see it in his eyes. The guy's name was Dewey Cass, and today Dewey is a national sales director with A. L. Williams. He's making a six-figure income, has nearly paid off that $150,000 debt, and is saving money.

Principle #4: *Desire becomes endurance.*

Once you've finally made a real commitment, desire becomes endurance. That's the extra ingredient I mentioned earlier.

A TV talk-show host once asked Pat Robertson about the grueling process that presidential hopefuls have to keep up in order to gather popular support. Robertson responded that each morning before he set off for the public appearances and speeches that filled his day, he asked God for endurance for that twenty-four-hour period. Endurance was the quality that Robertson felt he needed most to help him on his success path.

It's the same in business. Stop for a minute and think about this unwritten law:

UNWRITTEN LAW:	*The first eighteen months in business, everything turns into a mess.*

It's been my experience that it takes from three to five years to get a business—any business—off the ground. The first year and a half of that business, everything that can possibly go wrong will go wrong. If you don't have the quality of endurance, you might as well pack it up the first week.

Life isn't a sprint; it's a marathon. The ability to hang on when everything seems to be falling apart around you is a major difference between winners and losers.

Mel Fisher was a treasure hunter who believed a Spanish ship, the *Atocha,* had sunk somewhere off the coast of Florida. His only clue was a tiny bit of documentation that someone had stumbled across accidentally in a Spanish archive.

For sixteen years, Fisher searched for the ship, spending nearly $16 million. He found only a few artifacts near the surface of the ocean floor. Many people spoke out against Fisher's scant discoveries, saying that the artifacts were fake and that Fisher was just trying to recoup his losses. He got further and further into debt, but he refused to stop searching. There was tremendous pressure from his investors and the public to give up the search. His crew went sixteen weeks without a paycheck, continuing only because of Fisher's conviction.

During one expedition, Fisher's son, daughter-in-law, and another diver drowned. Still, he refused to give up. His philosophy continued to be "Today is the day!"

Ten years to the day after his son's death, Fisher found the *Atocha*. He was instantly wealthy and famous. The treasure has been estimated in the hundreds of millions, but it's priceless in terms of its historical and cultural value. It was the single largest treasure find ever.

It's necessary to have big dreams and big goals to succeed, but a dreamer without endurance is destined to fail. One of my favorite sayings is used by the Fellowship of Christian Athletes: "Dreamers are a dime a dozen, but marathoners are one in a million." Mel Fisher was a marathoner who got up every day saying, "Today is the day!" He simply refused to be discouraged, no matter how tough the odds.

It's true. And desire is the thing that will give you the endurance to run your marathon.

Gary Player won more international golf tournaments in his day than anyone else. Today, he's still winning on the senior tour.

When Player was competing in a tournament, people constantly came up to him and made the same remark: "I'd give anything if I could hit a golf ball like you."

On one particularly tough day, Player was tired and frustrated when, once again, he heard the comment: "I'd give anything if I could hit a golf ball like you."

Player's usual politeness failed him as he replied to the spectator, "No, you wouldn't. You'd give anything to hit a golf ball like me if it was easy. Do you know what you've got to do to hit a golf ball like me? You've got to get up at five o'clock in the morning, go out on the course, and hit one thousand golf balls. Your hand starts bleeding, and you walk up to the clubhouse, wash the blood off your hand, slap a bandage on it, and go out and hit another one thousand golf balls. That's what it takes to hit a golf ball like me."

I read a similar story recently. A famous violinist was approached by a woman who gushed, "I'd give my life to play like you do." The violinist responded simply, "Madam, I did."

Desire. It's the ingredient that causes people to devote their lives to a dream and keep moving toward it, no matter how tough. It's the intangible quality that has more impact on success than talent, education, or IQ. You can't see desire, but you can feel its presence and see its results in the lives of successful people.

All truly successful people have known the magic of desire. Decades ago, Abraham Lincoln gave this advice: "Always bear in mind that your own resolution to succeed is more important than any other one thing."

Former pro football player Jack Youngblood put it this way: "You learn that, whatever you are doing in life, obstacles don't matter very much. Pain or other circumstances can be there, but if you want to do a job bad enough, you'll find a way to get it done."

In our everyday lives, the message is there. We just put it more simply: "Where there's a will, there's a way."

CHAPTER FOUR

Warning: No Free Lunch

Opportunity is missed by most people because it is dressed in overalls and looks like work.
Thomas Edison

The next six chapters make up what I call "the six fundamentals to winning." After a lifetime of studying why some people win and others lose, I believe with everything that's in me that what all winners have in common is a mastery of these six areas.

But . . . before you can take advantage of these victory secrets, you *must* understand one critical point: You must understand the "magic formula" for winning, and you must master the fundamentals.

The "Magic Formula" for Winning

It's so simple that it's "revolutionary." The fact is, this formula, or principle, is misunderstood enough and overlooked enough that it can truly be called "magic" by those who understand it.

Ready? Here it is:

✔ You beat 50 percent of the people in America by working hard.

✔ You beat another 40 percent by being a person of honesty and integrity and standing for something.

✔ The last 10 percent is a dogfight in the free enterprise system.

I find that this simple concept is the hardest thing to get people to believe. But I know it's true. I've seen it time and time again.

Just take a minute and let it sink in. You beat 50 percent by working hard. I don't care if you're building a football team, going into business, starting a company, or running the country as its president, you beat 50 percent of the people *at any level* just by working hard consistently over a long period of time.

I get so mad when I read some of those get-rich-quick books on the market today. They talk about how you need to work smart, not hard, to succeed. Wrong! Nobody wants to tell you about the bone-wearing, back-breaking work it takes to succeed, but I can promise you one thing. You aren't going to get to square one if you aren't willing to work harder than you've ever worked in your life.

UNWRITTEN LAW:	*There is no "free lunch."*

Surprise! Work Isn't Fatal

I used to tell my football players that it was impossible to die from hard work. In the summer we'd have football camp, and we'd practice three times a day. I'd say, "Now, guys, you're going to get out there in the hot sun and you're going to be working and the coach is going to be fussing at you and you're going to feel like you're going to die. But when you feel like you're going to die, just keep working. Because the good Lord put a little mechanism in your head up there that makes you pass out before you die. If you do pass out, we'll drag you up to the dressing room and put you in the shower and give you some salt tablets, and you'll be ready for the next practice."

Of course, I was dedicated to my players and would never

have let anything happen to them. But that little speech was just a way of emphasizing the importance of really working hard. There's a lot of truth to it. I don't believe people die from hard work. They die from stress and worry and fear—the negative emotions. Those are the killers, not hard work. The fact is, in our society today, most people don't understand what hard work is all about.

Successful People Are Special—or Are They?

You know, when someone gets to be successful, everybody says, "Man, that guy was just born great. If I was like him, if I had his charisma (or background or style or speaking ability or whatever), I could be somebody."

That's one of the biggest myths about success. There's nothing more untrue.

Jerry Falwell is a great example of what hard work can produce. Today, Jerry is one of the most famous ministers in America. He is a friend and confidant to some of the most powerful people in the world. He has built one of the largest churches in the U.S. with over twenty thousand members. Each Sunday, five services are held just to accommodate the huge numbers of people that want to attend services at Thomas Road Baptist Church. Millions of people hear his message every week on television and radio.

People look at Jerry and say he was born great. But I can tell you that's not how his success happened. His first church was in a rundown Donald Duck Bottling Company building, acquired for $300 a month when that company went bankrupt. He had a building, but no members.

Jerry got up every morning at 5:30. At 6:30, he had a radio program, for which he paid $7 a day. Unlike the spectacular choir his church has today, Falwell's choir music came from a 45-rpm record. After the thirty-minute broadcast, he would go to his office and work until 9:00. Then he'd start knocking on doors. Every day, six days a week (not every other day or when he felt like it), Falwell knocked on one hundred doors, introducing himself and inviting people to his church. Usually, people just slammed the door in his face. But every sixtieth or seventieth time, someone would invite him in and allow him to talk about his new church. Today, buses pick up people to bring them to hear him preach, and his message reaches people all across America.

That's how Falwell built the international ministry he has today—through grueling work, every day, day in and day out, *one person at a time*. Falwell understood that there was no free lunch, and he didn't expect to succeed any way except through hard work.

Take a minute. Just think about knocking on one hundred doors a day for six days a week and then preaching two sermons on Sunday and doing a radio broadcast every day. That's unreal!

Now, people look at me like I always had it made, too. Nothing could be further from the truth. My first two years in the business, I was dying every day. I've got the kind of personality that makes me want everyone to like me and agree with me. I just couldn't face the rejection. When I started out, I wanted to quit every single day—not every other day—for *two* years!

My sixth year in the business, I was still just making a living, $30,000 or so, and I was working six days a week. Everyone kept telling me I was crazy. They told me it wasn't worth it. They said I should give up and return to coaching. But I had such a burning desire, I couldn't stand being average and ordinary. I hung in there, and just four years later I was a millionaire.

Most people don't give themselves enough time. You've got to work hard, not for a few weeks or a few months, but for a few years. It takes three to five years to establish yourself in business. The first two years of any business are nothing but survival time. (Remember the unwritten law that the first eighteen months in business, everything turns into a mess.)

Even after you're doing well, you've got to keep working hard if you want to get better and keep your business growing and developing until you make it big. If you *are* willing to work hard, you've already beaten 50 percent of the people in America. At least half the people out there just don't want it bad enough to work that hard.

You can beat another 40 percent by living right and standing for something. I don't mean being perfect. I mean trying to live a decent, moral life and finding something to believe in.

Most people roll out of bed every morning, and they don't have any purpose in life. You've got to find something that you can commit to (more about this later) and then live a decent life.

Understand, you beat 90 percent of the people—no matter what problems and shortcomings you have—90 percent—just by working hard and being a person of integrity with strong beliefs!

That last 10 percent is a dogfight because 10 percent of the people are going to be as tough as you are. And that's the way it should be in the free enterprise system.

Master the Fundamentals

Fundamentals are the key to winning. I'm often frustrated in my business life that so many people don't realize that. It doesn't matter how intelligent you are. One thing I've discovered in business is that the smartest people in the world make some of the same mistakes as the not-so-smart people. The biggest mistake *everybody* makes is not recognizing the importance of fundamentals.

You Win With Fundamentals

A lot of people search for a system that guarantees success, but a system isn't the key. It's just like in football. The teams use different systems: Oklahoma wins with the "wishbone"; Nebraska wins with the "I-formation"; South Carolina wins with the "run and shoot"; Tennessee wins with the "pro set"; Miami wins with the "pass"; and Georgia wins with the "run."

The winning team is the team that is better at blocking and tackling and is in better condition physically and mentally than its opponent. The team wins because the players have mastered the fundamentals of the game.

The Greatest "Master" of the Fundamentals

Coach Paul "Bear" Bryant was one of my heroes and, I believe, the greatest football coach who ever lived. A look at Coach Bryant's record shows that he won big everywhere he went. He went to Maryland, Kentucky, Texas A&M, and Alabama—those were his four head coaching jobs—and each of those schools had a losing team before he went there.

When Coach Bryant took over, he started with the same players, the same facilities, and the same alumni as each coach before him. All of a sudden, there was a different atmosphere, a different way of doing things. At each school, almost immediately things began to improve. Before long, Coach Bryant's teams were dominating teams everywhere they went. A lot of people say, "Well, Coach Bryant was just an absolute genius. He knew more about football, about systems and plays than anyone else."

Dead wrong!

Coach Bum Phillips of the New Orleans Saints, who was Coach Bryant's assistant coach in his early years, has described what made Coach Bryant different: "Other coaches coach football; Coach Bryant coaches people."

I believe that. I've been to coaching clinics and heard Coach Bryant speak. As you listened to him, you realized that he knew a lot about football, but he didn't know that much more about the technical aspects of football than other coaches. You look at the players he had on his winning teams, and they were not all that much bigger or stronger than other college football players.

What Was Coach Bryant's Secret?

But there was a difference in the way Coach Bryant looked at people, the way he understood what made people tick. He understood, better than anyone I've ever seen, the fundamentals of winning. As Coach Jake Gaither of Florida A&M put it, "Coach Bryant could take his and beat yours and take yours and beat his."

What that means more than anything else is that Coach Bryant was different; he was unique. He knew something about coaching that nobody else knew. He knew how to coach *people,* and the technique he used was coaching the fundamentals of the game.

You know, the difference between winning and being average and ordinary is so small, it's almost unbelievable. You can do 99 percent of the things right and not do the little things that are the key to winning, and you're guaranteed to fail. This little edge that I talk about is a special kind of mental toughness. I think of it as a winning edge. It all comes down to fundamentals—the fundamentals of winning.

When I took my first head coaching job, I learned a great lesson. For the two years before that, I had been assistant coach at a great football school, Thomasville High School in Thomasville, Georgia. Thomasville had a dominant football team. Everything about the football program was first-class. We had great players, we had great facilities, we had great coaches and a great program, and Thomasville won year in and year out.

Then I left that job and went to my first head coaching job. My new team had won only one game in two years and hadn't had a winning season in probably twenty years.

I went in thinking that everything was really the same. It was the same size school as Thomasville; they played in the same league in Georgia (one of the best). So when I went in there as head coach, I was going to coach just like I had coached at Thomasville.

Boy, was I in for a shock. The players didn't know the fundamentals of the game. I had to start teaching the kids the basics—how to get down in a stance, how to block a dummy, how to hold a football, how to tackle, and on and on. I don't mind telling you that I was worried.

The kids were small, and they were weak. I went out and bought some weights. I did anything I could think of to work on the fundamentals—and to get the kids to believe in themselves.

You already know that I believe attitude is everything. Well, with their football record, those kids naturally didn't have great attitudes. I started telling the kids that we were a team of destiny, that nobody expected us to win and we were going to slip up on somebody and surprise the whole world.

You know what? That next football year, we were 7–3. We upset the number-one team in the state, and I was voted Coach of the Year. We did shock the whole state, and our team was almost as surprised as everyone else!

That experience proved to me another unwritten law that I've lived by ever since:

UNWRITTEN LAW: *Inch by inch, it's a cinch.*

Our little team looked like a mess at the beginning of the year, but because the players worked on fundamentals, every day, one day at a time, that whole program turned around.

Another Team That Won—by "Inches"

When we started A. L. Williams, we were competing against big giants in American business, such as Prudential, New York Life, and Northwestern Mutual. These companies spent millions of dollars on advertising, and they had everything you would think you had to have to win.

We started A. L. Williams with eighty-five people. We had no money, no name. It was hard to find somebody to take our business. We had little support. There was no reason to think that we could compete with the giants in our business. But I had learned back in coaching that fundamentals were the key and that inch by inch, it's a cinch.

You don't go in, snap your fingers, and instantly step into a winning situation. If you haven't been winning or you're going out and getting your first opportunity, you're not going to snap your fingers and all of a sudden be competing with the giants—

or all of a sudden be making giant income or having giant success.

That's just not the way it is. You've got to understand that you've got to make an eight-to-ten-year commitment. You've got to understand that the first year and a half, everything you touch does fall apart. It takes from three to five years just to establish a business where you're consistently doing the right things, where you consistently compete.

The way you win and build a dominating team (like Coach Bryant did) or build a dominating business where you become financially independent and produce a lot of other successful people is by doing it one step at a time. You've got to master these fundamentals, and then you've got to work at it. You look at it, and it looks totally impossible. When you look at the giants in your business, winning may seem like a pipe dream.

In our industry, Prudential and some of the other giants had been in business for one hundred years. These were some of the most powerful, well-known companies in America. We were challenging, really, an institution and these big, powerful companies used every competitive edge they had. There was no way a reasonable-thinking human being who sat down and drew out a business plan could logically think that we could survive, much less build a national championship company.

But the way you build a national championship team is inch by inch. Rather than look at the things the competition had and the things we didn't have and get depressed, we concentrated on the six fundamentals.

The Fundamentals

I believed then, and I still do, that the way you build a championship group in any area—a championship football team, a championship family, or a champion business—is by mastering these six fundamentals:

1. Become a dreamer again.

2. Have a crusade.
3. Dream big—but keep it simple.
4. Always be positive.
5. Treat people "good."
6. Never give up.

I found out that you can't spend your life comparing yourself to everybody else, especially people who have already made it, because that builds tremendous depression in you and a feeling of hopelessness. You've got to understand what you've got to do to win, and the key is fundamentals. If you'll make a long-term commitment (eight to ten years), and you'll say, "Now, I'm going to start working in these six areas," you're ahead of the pack. You might not be good right now in your positive attitude. You've been negative because you've been dumped on so many times. But you've got to try.

You're not going to snap your fingers overnight and suddenly be positive, either. You've got to understand it's inch by inch. You've got to change slowly over a period of time.

You've got to work at it constantly. You're going to say, "Today, I'm going to go out and be positive." And you're going to go to work and you might be positive for a few minutes or a few hours and then, all of a sudden, your past is going to come back to haunt you. You're going to fall into your old trap again. What you've got to do is give yourself a pep talk. You've got to say, "I want to win. I want to be somebody. I'm failing in this area, and I've got to go to work. That's what winners do." Inch by inch, it's a cinch.

More than 90 percent of all new companies fail their first two or three years. Our goal at A. L. Williams was to dominate the largest industry in America, to beat companies that had been established in business for over one hundred years. It looked impossible. We started in three states with eight offices. But we started on the fundamentals, inch by inch, getting better and better every day. Just like Coach Bryant, we started building people.

Today, we're recruiting thousands of people a month. Back then, we were recruiting maybe five people a month. But that's where you have to start. You can't just say, "Boy, I wish we were recruiting ten thousand people a month." Start with what you've got, and you start getting better. You must have a goal of getting better every day.

Today, we're producing over one hundred vice presidents every month. Our first year in A. L. Williams, we produced one vice president that whole year. You can't sit there and say, "I wish I was as big as Prudential. I wish I was as big as New York Life." We took those eighty-five people and those five or ten or fifteen recruits we were bringing in every month, and we started working with them. We said we were a company of destiny. We knew we were doing something right, and we were going to make a tremendous impact on the largest industry in the world. We were going to beat Prudential, and we started building on that.

And just six years later, we did it. We became the number-one seller of individual life insurance in America, more than Prudential, New York Life, or anyone else.

YOU Are the Key

If you haven't won up to this point in your life, it's time to wake up and realize that nobody is going to strike an oil well in your back yard. Nobody is going to knock on your door and say, "Here's your opportunity. I name you president of the company." That doesn't happen to people that look like you and me and come from where we come from.

You've got to change; you've got to do something in the future that's different from what you've done in the past. That's a fact you must accept before you can get started.

Now, I know you're probably saying, "Baloney!"

Well, all I can say to you is "Go look in the mirror." Go look at that man or woman and think about the last five years or six years. I can promise you that if you don't change, the next five or six are going to be exactly the same.

Now, ain't that depressing?

Get Fundamentally Sound—and Stay Fundamentally Sound

If you're ready to accept responsibility for your life and start changing the patterns of the past, you've got to master the six fundamentals of winning given in the next few chapters.

You can't just read about them and then go on to something else. You've got to study and apply them in your life. You need to think about them every day. Every time you have a disappointment, go back and say, "Where am I weak? Which one of these fundamentals did I forget?" Nine times out of ten, the reason things aren't working is that you forgot one or more of the fundamentals to winning.

If you're ready to work, get ready for the fundamentals that will make your hard work pay off!

Do it!

CHAPTER FIVE

Become a Dreamer Again

The future belongs to those who believe in the beauty of their dreams.

Eleanor Roosevelt

Stop for a minute and catch your breath. For these few pages, stop thinking with your brain and think with your heart. Use that mysterious thing called "imagination."

First, *make a wish.*

Fun, isn't it? And it's easy. In fact, it's so easy, so simple, so natural, that you've probably never given it much thought. But, you know what?

It's the inspiration for winning.

Dreaming.

You're probably saying, "Art, this time you've really lost it. What does dreaming have to do with success?"

The truth is, dreams are one of the most powerful success tools you have. Now, I'll say something even more outrageous. My message in this chapter is "make whatever wish you dare, and it will come true."

I'm serious. I believe with everything that's in me that whatever you dream about, you can achieve.

How is this possible? Because if desire is the secret to winning, as I said earlier, dreaming is the secret of desire. *Dreams are the fuel that fire desire.*

UNWRITTEN LAW: *If you don't have a big dream, you're dead.*

The thing that gives Napoleon Hill's book, *Think and Grow Rich,* believability is his research. He studied a number of successful people, and the one common cord running through them was that they were dreamers. They were just burning up inside with a dream they had cherished for years.

Folks, it's impossible to do anything great without a big dream. If you don't have a big dream, you're dead. Not physically, of course, but your opportunity to "be somebody" is dead.

But by the same token, anyone (even you!) can have a big dream.

And anyone (even you!) who is a dreamer can still win.

And anyone (yes, you, too!) can begin to change in thirty days, beginning with the power of a dream.

Stop thinking about how hopeless your situation is right now. Start thinking about the power of dreams.

Then go ahead and *make a wish.*

Some Who Dared to Dream

Let's look at a few dreamers and see how they "beat the odds":

THE DREAM

THE DREAMER

An eccentric inventor and drifter witnesses the deaths of a number of children who drank contaminated milk. He dreams of finding a way to preserve milk.

Gail Borden
Borden's Milk & Ice Cream

A widower with a young son loses his job at a department store. He dreams of being his own boss and scrapes together $1,500 to open his own store.

George Kinney
Kinney Shoes

A six-year-old boy dreams of a way to make chicken eggs hatch faster. His solution is to sit on the eggs himself. It is the first glimmer of his genius and the start of ideas that would change the world.

Thomas Alva Edison
Inventor: light bulb, phonograph player, motion picture

Growing up, a little girl likes to touch people's faces and comb their hair. She loves helping people make themselves pretty, and she dreams of becoming a skin care specialist while she watches her uncle cook up creams and potions on her mother's gas stove.

Estēe Lauder
Estēe Lauder Cosmetics and Skin Care Products

Two tinkerers set up shop in the garage of one of their homes with the dream of being on the leading edge of technology. One of their first inventions is an electronic harmonica tuner.

William Hewlett and *David Packard*
Hewlett-Packard Information Systems

Living in a government-funded housing project in Pennsylvania, he dreams of escaping the mines of his home state. A good athlete, he knows sports.

Mike Ditka
Pro football player; head coach of Chicago Bears

Two brothers-in-law have a simple dream of starting a business together and making $75 a week. They have a brilliantly simple marketing philosophy: one product served thirty-one different ways.

Burton Baskin and *Irvine Robbins*
Baskin-Robbins Ice Cream

In the 1800s, many surgery patients die from infections caused by unsanitary conditions. A young dreamer convinces his brothers to work with him to find a way to produce sterile bandages.

Robert, Edward, and *James Johnson*
Johnson & Johnson Health Care Products

After his older brother is shot down and killed in World War II, this teenager listens to the radio to ease his loneliness, and he dreams of someday being an announcer on his own show.

Dick Clark
"American Bandstand"

A general practitioner dreams of performing a surgical procedure thought by everyone to be impossible. His goal is to achieve this dream before rheumatoid arthritis prevents him from operating.

Dr. Christiaan Barnard
First successful human heart transplant

HALT! Don't Get Discouraged

Now, I know what you're thinking. You've just read about these incredible dreamers, and you're thinking, *But I'm not like that.* Don't get discouraged! You need to dream big, but remember that you can always "expand" your dream. In her talks across the country, Angela reminds listeners of her favorite Zig Ziglar quote, "Dream as far as you can see, and when you get there, you can see farther." Angela tells how I have expanded my dreams over the years as I have grown. She says I started out wanting financial security for my family. Then I wanted to be financially independent. Then I wanted to build the number-one life insurance sales organization in the country, and so on. So if you can't relate to some far-off dream, bring it down just a little closer.

I have a friend who lives in California, and I think we all can relate to him. Jim Minor was the kind of guy we've all worked with. He was a "company man" who had worked hard for twenty-one years as the parts manager of a Chrysler dealership. He was valuable to the department and had even helped build its revenues. In return, his employer would raise his income by about $1,000 every so often.

Jim felt good about his accomplishments, but he was still a little disappointed. He had a dream of doing something special with his life, but he couldn't seem to find the right vehicle. He had tried a lot of things, but it seemed like something always went wrong. He thought he had found an opportunity in silver, but when the silver market went down the tubes, so did Jim's hopes.

Jim began to feel like most of us do, that time was running

out. He was forty-four, with a wife and two children. He had known tragedy; a child by a former marriage had committed suicide. His health was starting to fail. His blood pressure was almost out of control, even with the medication his doctor had prescribed. One of his friends described him at the time as "forty-four, going on seventy."

But he kept dreaming, never giving up hope that there was something better for Jim Minor.

When one of our leaders mentioned our business to an acquaintance, the guy immediately thought of Jim. At the risk of being fired if he was caught exploring another job, Jim talked to our vice president.

But even Jim's friends weren't encouraging. One of them told our vice president that although Jim was a great guy, he just wasn't going to amount to anything.

At first, it did look a little doubtful. Jim was so scared and so nervous that he couldn't talk to people. On one client call with his manager, his hands shook so hard (even though he wasn't giving the presentation!) that his manager had to whisper to him to put them under the table. Hoping to build his confidence, his manager asked him to give a small, informal presentation to a group of five or six other sales reps. When the manager talked to Jim's wife, he discovered that Jim hadn't slept for two days before the meeting.

In a lot of ways, the whole thing was a miserable experience for Jim. But he kept showing up for work, putting the key in the door, working late into the night, never taking a day off.

Today, Jim Minor is a senior vice president with a solid organization and a big income. He and his wife, Deanna, have traveled with our company all over the world. He's a long way from the parts business. Even his health has improved; he no longer has the erratic blood pressure that came from a constant feeling of frustration and failure.

I love Jim's story because it's not an "instant success" story. It's a story of constant struggle and countless obstacles. Jim had every reason to feel that life had passed him by, but he never gave up on his dream. He's living proof that you can become what you dream.

Forget That Dreams Are "Kid's Stuff"

In the first chapter of this book, I talked about the dreams of childhood. I gave you some responses of a fifth-grade class in a public school in Georgia. To come up with the answers, the teacher asked the children to write what they wanted to be when they grew up on a piece of paper and pass it to the front of the room. Now, put yourself in that teacher's place for a moment. She has spent almost six months with the same twenty-five children, day in and day out. She knows who has made A's all year and who has made C's. She knows who the parents of these children are and what kind of home environment they come from. She has a really good idea which of these children society would select as "the achievers" and which society would brand as "the losers." Yet, all twenty-five children, every single one, responded with a big dream. Not just a little dream. I'm talking *big dream*. Their minds were filled with possibilities. Isn't that incredible?

Isn't it great that the kid living in the worst slums, whose parents are financially destitute, who seemingly doesn't have much of a chance in the world, can say, "When I grow up, I'm going to be a doctor or an astronaut," with just as much conviction and belief as the kid from the richest, most privileged family in America? They don't know what "privileged" is; they just know about desire.

Folks, the most bankrupt people in the world are the ones who've lost their ability to dream. As we become adults, "reality" sets in. We discover that the world doesn't revolve around us, and we begin to lose those big dreams. They seem so far away, so unattainable. It becomes harder and harder to gather up the self-esteem we need to believe that our dreams are possible.

For some people, it's disaster. They get so low that they think they're no good for anything. They can't even remember what it was like to have hopes and dreams. Pretty soon, they can't even get up in the morning. In extreme cases, they just quit.

Most of us have been in cities where we've seen bag ladies or winos sleeping on subway grates or derelicts camping out under overpasses. Even after you pass them, you just can't seem to get them off your mind. My heart goes out to these people. I think it's the saddest thing on earth. They've given up. Life doesn't even seem worth living. These are the truly bankrupt people in America.

I realize that this is pretty serious stuff, maybe even a little depressing. But I think it's critical for you to see that you're dead inside if you have no big dream.

Even if you're not the extreme case, you're probably somewhere in between. But that is still a danger zone. Most of us are just comfortable enough to kind of drift along, existing from day to day. We still have some hopes and dreams, but they're scaled down considerably from what they were when we were younger.

These scaled-down dreams just aren't good enough. You'll never "be somebody" by just drifting along. If you're going to be successful, you need to pause right now, and throw out the idea that dreams are kid's stuff. You've got to do it. You may feel stupid. You may not want to admit it to anybody. But it's critical if you want to win. I promise.

Rewards of Dreaming, Competing, and Winning

I'd love it if there were some way people could experience firsthand the feeling you get when you accomplish your dreams. I wish they had a machine or something that people could step into and experience that feeling—just for one minute or one hour. Do you know why I say that?

UNWRITTEN LAW: *As great as you think your dream will be when you reach it, it will always be one thousand times better.*

As great as I thought being financially independent would be, I found out it was one thousand times better. I sat back and said, "Man, if I had known it was going to be this good, I would have been willing to pay twice as big a price."

If one of your dreams is financial independence, I hope you've thought about all the ways it could change your life. It has allowed me to do things for people who are special to me, and this alone gives me an indescribable feeling. Let's look at some of the rewards of dreaming, competing, and winning.

Provide for Your Parents

The older we get, the more most of us appreciate the tremendous price our parents paid to provide for us when we were young. We would give anything to be able to return some of that in ways other than just love and affection. In our company, many of our successful people feel that repaying their parents has been one of the greatest rewards of financial independence.

National Sales Director Greg Fitzpatrick was a high-school basketball coach. He had a dream come true when he was able to take his parents along on a family trip to England, something he never could have afforded otherwise. Former policeman Neal Askew is another of our top leaders who helped his parents and his in-laws to afford new homes. My wife, Angela, saw a dream come true when we were able to build a library on the campus of Cairo High School, the high school where we both grew up. She was able to dedicate the building to her parents who are both still living—a once-in-a-lifetime dream.

But perhaps the story of the wife of one of our national sales directors says it better than any of them. Teresa Crossland was six years old and her sister was two when their father died of a heart attack. Teresa's dad didn't have much in the way of life insurance, and what little he had was quickly eaten up by medical bills and funeral expenses. In Montgomery, Alabama, there weren't many opportunities for a thirty-eight-year-old widow. The future looked pretty dismal.

Teresa's grandparents moved in with them to take care of

the girls while her mother got a job to support her "new" family of five. Her mother worked several jobs at one time, and she even started a portrait business with a friend. With her income, Teresa's mother was able to provide for the family, and while money was hard won, the home had a lot of love and pride.

Teresa fondly recalls how her mother tried to do things, in a modest way, that would be special treats for the children. "One summer, my mother rented a hotel room for the weekend in downtown Montgomery so we could swim in the pool and eat out in the restaurant," she says.

It was painful, sometimes, for Teresa and her family not to be able to afford a "real" vacation or a new dress or the "in" kind of clothing, but money had to be well spent, not squandered.

Through their frugal lifestyle, the help of a student loan, and a handful of part-time jobs, Teresa graduated from college. She became a high-school teacher, and it was then that her life took a big turn. She met and married Rusty Crossland, a high-school basketball coach making $10,000 a year. The newlyweds started out with nothing—nothing, that is, but their dreams. Rusty and Teresa believed there was something better for their family than just getting by. When Rusty joined our company, he and Teresa wanted to be financially independent. Today, Rusty and Teresa are millionaires.

Guess what the rewards have been for Teresa?

The Crosslands live in a restored farmhouse and raise horses as a hobby. Their children go to private school, and they take exciting family vacations. But most of all, Teresa has been able to show her mother how much she appreciates all the sacrifices she made. Three years ago, Teresa bought her mother a new car. But when she comes to visit, Teresa's mother doesn't drive; Teresa sends her a plane ticket. She's also helped her mother remodel her home and has taken her on vacations to Hawaii and Lake Tahoe.

What is your dream? You'd better find out. For Rusty and Teresa, it made all the difference in the world.

Help Others with Medical Debts

A former high-school teacher, basketball coach, and one of our national sales directors recently spent over $75,000 in medical costs for her sister. She had become paralyzed last year because of an aneurysm, and the family never would have been able to provide some special help for her rehabilitation if it had not been for the NSD's financial situation. Mike Wooten, another national sales director with our company, has a grandmother who required triple bypass surgery. Mike was able to bring the entire family to a hotel nearby and provide for their expenses during her surgery and recovery period.

Support Charities

Former railroad engineer Hubert Humphrey used part of his income to be the sole sponsor for a member of his church who left on a two-year mission. Former high-school basketball coach Bill Whittle and his family realized a dream come true when, because of their tithing, the church was able to completely pay off the mortgage, freeing up more money for church missions.

Virginia Carter is the single parent of four children, and the welfare of her young ones has always been her first concern. She would pay any price to make a good life for them. Today, she is one of the most respected leaders in our company. She is a national sales director and a millionaire, and one of her greatest pleasures is being able to make contributions to children's organizations. For Ginny, the rewards of financial independence have been sweet.

Help Humankind

We all hurt inside when we hear about global problems such as nuclear disasters, guerrilla war, famine, child abuse, and many other problems that seem too big for any one of us, as individuals, to cope with. However, financial independence often puts people in the position of helping with these problems. Mike Sharpe and Doug Hartman, two of our national sales director in California, were able to use their financial resources to help fight child pornography in their state. Many others have devoted time, energy, and financial assistance to help in the battle against world hunger and other critical problems. For any individual, just being able to help in these areas is one of the most important rewards of success.

How to Strengthen Your Dreams

Once you know your dreams, there are other things you can do to help you hold on to them and keep them from being pushed aside by the demands of daily life.

Learn to Visualize

A big obstacle you face is visualizing yourself in another role—the role of a successful person. For me, I had to see myself as someone who could make money and become financially independent. You've got to look at yourself as someone with possibilities in your life, not certainties. You've got to *see yourself winning.*

A couple of years ago, I pulled into our home office parking lot, and one of our Atlanta division leaders was walking back to his car. We spoke to each other, and as he pulled away in his car, I noticed his license plate read "RVP 2 B." Translated, that tag meant "Regional Vice President to Be." You know what? That guy reached his goal of RVP later that year.

Monte Holm came from a family of fourteen children in Utah. His family was so poor, their home had plastic over the windows instead of glass. When Monte looked at our company, he was very young, in his early twenties. He was told by a number of people that his chances of making it big in A. L. Williams were a thousand to one, primarily because of his age and where he lived at the time. But he refused to listen. Instead, Monte had heard a speech about visualizing goals and dreams. He wrote his dreams down on paper, about ten pages of them, and read his list every day. The yellow pages in the legal pad became dog-eared and crumpled from use. Today, Monte owns his own business with A. L. Williams, a business that now has revenues of over $500,000 a year. He still reads his goals and says he has missed only ten or eleven days of reading them in the last eight years.

Larry Sternberg is another great dreamer in our company. Larry was a drugstore manager making $17,000 when he first committed himself to dreaming nine years ago. His goal was more than just to be his own boss; Larry wanted to be financially independent. Today, he is well on his way to that dream, but he and his wife, Karen, have a new goal in sight—a beautiful dream home. To give him added incentive, Larry has put a tiny model of the home on the desk in his office where he can see it every day. Larry has set a goal of saving $1 million in cash, and once he achieves that, they will pour the foundation for the new home. I have no doubt that Larry will make it.

Every day, visualize yourself winning, even if you haven't decided on the path you want to go. Sit down for a few minutes each day and close your eyes. See yourself the way you want to be. Visualize yourself owning your own business or changing your job. See yourself paying off all your bills every month and having money left over. See yourself with $50,000 in your savings account or $100,000 or whatever your goal is.

Of all the people who knew how to visualize their dreams, Walt Disney is perhaps the greatest. After he had his business in Hollywood going, he created a staff of people called the "Imagineers." These creative people would help Disney put his dreams of Disneyland and motion pictures down on paper. Once others could see what he envisioned, they became excited, too. His ultimate dream was EPCOT, a center for a community of ideas and research. The inspiration of the Imagineers enabled EPCOT to be completed, even after Disney's death in 1966. You achieve what you envision. What you see, you become.

Involve Your Family in Your Dreams

A dream has a greater chance of becoming a reality if it's shared by other family members, especially your spouse. The best dreams are the ones built by two people. Talk about your dream; go over the steps of your goal with your spouse and kids. Put the goals in writing someplace that your family will see often—maybe on the door of the refrigerator. Talk about how you're doing. Besides giving them a sense of involvement, you may be surprised at the support and encouragement you get. When you fall short, they can remind you of your goals and urge you on.

For a couple of years, my daughter worked at our company. Whenever I got down on myself or negative, she was the first to remind me of what I always say about a positive attitude. She'd tell me how great I was, how special I was. How could I be discouraged with that kind of support?

I believe my wife, Angela, is the most perfect partner a person could ever have. As our lives have changed, she has changed her role in supporting our dreams. When I first started my business, she continued to teach so that we would have a secure form of income until my business got going. Later, she left teaching and came into the office to be my office manager, secretary, and anything else I needed.

When I started traveling and our children were still in junior high and high school, she would stay home to make sure they had a great home environment. After the children were grown, she began traveling with me. Today, she has built a tremendous network of the spouses of our agents called the Partners Organization. The sole purpose of this organization is to offer support to the families of our agents and to teach the families how they can share in the dreams of A. L. Williams.

Angela was there, every step of the way, supporting my dream. Without her constant support, both in the tough early years of the company and today, my future would have been very different. The bottom line: it's much easier to be motivated when you know your spouse and your kids are behind you.

Find an Environment That Encourages You to Dream

Most of the people reading this book probably aren't interested in the same career I had. Your dream may not be to own your own business. Sales or marketing may not be your niche. Whatever area you work in to achieve your dream, finding an environment that encourages you to dream can make a big difference. I'm no fan of corporate America, but even in the corporate world, some companies encourage people to dream big.

Bob Turley is a close personal friend of mine. He was one of the original seven vice presidents in our company. All of you sports fans my age know that Bob Turley was a star pitcher for the New York Yankees. He played with them in seven World Series games. He was a Cy Young Award winner and also received the Hickok belt. Bob Turley is one of those people who just can't stand being average and ordinary. He would be a winner no matter where he was.

One of Bob's strengths has been knowing the importance of an environment that encourages dreaming. To illustrate his point, he makes a great analogy between the business world and the world of professional baseball. Bob says that very few people start out as successes in baseball, but that is their dream—to become a professional baseball player. When they're just starting out, they don't have the talent, training, or experience to survive in the majors. So baseball has the league system. That system sorts out who is good enough for the major leagues, based purely on ability.

Everybody starts out in the minor leagues because the system understands that if you put a player in the majors before he's ready, he'll be sure to fail. Instead, they start players with talent at the minor league level. They build up the players' confidence by having them play against people at their own ability level.

Every player is judged on talent alone. It doesn't matter what his background is or who he knows. Every player is encouraged to give his best, to reach for the stars, to push the limits of his own ability. He's able to compare himself to the other players to see how he stacks up. Most players quickly get a sense of whether they have enough talent to make it.

In that system, nobody loses. The players are encouraged to dream of a great baseball career. That's why they're there.

They are allowed to go out and pay the price and compete. The very best players are picked for the majors. It's true that not everybody makes it. But even if the players don't make it to the majors, they've been encouraged to give it their best shot. They've had the chance to go for their dreams. Even the players who don't make it can go away from the experience without the bitterness and disillusionment that so many people have about their careers. They got a chance in an environment that believed in their right to dream of being the best.

Whatever You Dream About, You Can Become

You know, I talked earlier about how much I hated the sales business. I didn't hate it just sometimes, but every minute from the time I left coaching. I hated all those rejections, the pressure of asking people to let you see them, everything about sales. I guess I can't say enough about how much I wanted to quit and go back to coaching and a salaried income. I wanted a principal who would tell me my working hours were 8:00 to 4:00. In the insurance business, I saw many people quit. I'd see them later, and they'd say, "Man, you must be crazy. You're a madman to stay in that business. You don't make nearly enough money to be working as hard as you're working." (I was making about $30,000 at the time.) You think that didn't affect me? I worked so hard, I felt like a public nuisance (I probably was!). I'd wake up every morning just dreading going into that office. It was bad.

But I had a dream.

And that dream was to own my own business and to gain financial security for my family. I couldn't do that by coaching. So I held on. And no matter how scared I was of getting another "no," I'd make one more sale; I'd recruit one more person. I knew if I followed my plan, I'd make it.

I have so much love and admiration for the people who started our company. It takes people with the hearts of giants to withstand some of the ridicule they took, just because they were dreamers. There they were, a bunch of teachers, coaches, firemen, and policemen who held meetings in each other's houses and talked about how one day they would be among the highest paid people in their community. The odds of that coming true were probably a fraction of 1 percent. But in their hearts, they believed they could do it. It was their dream, and no one could take that away from them.

Bill Anderton was one of those people who held fast to his dream. He had come from a humble background in Jackson, Mississippi, where he lived with his mother and stepfather. Bill's stepfather was a truck mechanic who made modest wages and firmly believed that "big dreams" were for foolish men, and he preached to Bill the doctrine of hard work. On occasion, Bill would visit his real father, who was a high risk taker, always looking for a get-rich-quick scheme. Bill's father was either "in the money" and rubbing shoulders with successful people or flat broke. Bill remembers his favorite phrase, "We're just one deal away from a big home, a swimming pool, and a Cadillac."

As Bill grew older, he perceptively realized that while neither man's method was effective, there was value in both. He worked hard and put himself through college, but he also planned for the day when he would have the financial resources to make goals like those of his father's come true.

Bill has been with our company for ten years, and despite his humble roots, he has achieved his goals.

Several years ago, a wealthy man in Bill's hometown built a beautiful home in a prestigious neighborhood. Recently, he went bankrupt, and the bank had to take back the home and mortgage. One of the executives called Bill because he knew Bill was one person who could afford such an estate.

Today, Bill is living in that dream house, but a few years ago, he was a dreamer nobody believed. He was a high-school basketball coach, never supposed to "make it big" in the business world. But because of his ability to dream, Bill changed the course of his life.

Only in the free enterprise system can this happen. Folks, that's exactly where you live, in the free enterprise system. I'm willing to bet that your situation in life is not much different from the way Bill started out.

Do you have a dream? Do you believe it can happen? Whatever you dream about, you can become.

CHAPTER SIX

Have a Crusade

Strong lives are motivated by dynamic purposes.
Kenneth Hildebrand

Did you ever wonder why so many famous people seem to lead unhappy lives? Everywhere you look, magazines and books tell stories of the heartbreaks of the rich and famous. They're checking into drug and alcohol rehabilitation centers; their third or fourth or fifth marriages are breaking up; their families are in a mess.

These people managed to fulfill their dreams—of being a movie idol, a great entertainer, or a rock star. They had the desire and the determination to stick it out until they reached their dream. Yet when they made it to the top, they were still unhappy. Their success didn't give them the instant satisfaction that they thought it would.

Why Money Doesn't Buy Happiness

I've got a theory about why that happens. Remember how we talked earlier about how little kids think they're the center of the universe? Well, some people never outgrow that way of thinking. All their lives they are obsessed by what *they* want; all their hopes and dreams concern themselves and nobody else. I know some people like that, and they've been very successful. But of the hundreds of successful people I've studied and observed, the people who've been the most successful—not just in terms of financial success, but in their quality of life—were the crusaders.

Why should you have a crusade? There are two important reasons.

1. *A crusade adds meaning and purpose to your life.*

You can make it with just a personal dream, and a lot of people do. But most people perform at their best when they're a part of something bigger than themselves. Remember little Jessica McClure who fell into the well in Texas? People from all over that area worked to save her. As the word spread, people who didn't even know the little girl or her family willingly spent dozens of hours without sleep, away from their own homes, even risked their lives to help rescue her. For two and a half days, in homes all across America, people were glued to their TV sets as they waited in breathtaking suspense, then joy, as the eighteen-month-old child was lifted out of the well.

People need to see themselves involved as *active participants* in some great event. It's a need just like food and shelter. Life is richer when our efforts reach beyond our doorstep.

2. *Crusaders die hard.*

People who have a crusade have an extra edge in life. They hang on to their dreams when the rest of us would get tired and stop. They have inner strength and toughness that can't be duplicated in any other way. A dream backed up by a crusade is an almost unstoppable combination.

A crusade gives you something to fight for. When we were first starting our company, a young single guy was a crusader for term insurance like you wouldn't believe. In his town the traditional insurance industry was firmly entrenched. A few unscrupulous agents did just about everything you can imagine to discourage him from continuing his business. His tires were slashed, rocks were thrown at the house, and once, a snake was even placed in his mailbox to scare the family.

The strain was sometimes intense; I'm not sure if I could have stood it. But the tougher things got, the more committed he became. He was going to run his business and do what he felt was right for consumers. He refused to be defeated. He hung on, and it paid off. Today, eleven years later, he and his family (a lovely wife and four little girls) live a happy life. His courage and determination enabled him to win in a big way; he has a beautiful home in that same community and enjoys financial independence.

Much of the progress in our country has come from men and women who had more than a business—they had a crusade to make a better product, a cheaper product, a product that made life easier or more pleasant.

When Henry Ford came on the scene, automobiles were luxury items available only to the rich. He had a crusade to make automobiles cheaply enough that every American family could own one. Henry Ford became a multimillionaire, and today, the Ford Motor Company is one of the great companies in American business.

Tom Monaghan, with many other business ventures behind him, opened a pizza parlor with $900 of borrowed money. His crusade was simple—to offer people the convenience of a hot pizza, delivered to their door. Today, the name "Domino's" is synonymous with home-delivered pizza, and his company has annual revenues in excess of $1 billion.

A. T. Cross wanted to make an ink pen and a mechanical pencil that would last a lifetime. His manufacturing process involved pulling any pen or pencil that production workers even suspected of having a flaw. In the firm's entire history, only 2 percent of customers have ever returned a pen to the company for repairs. Today, Cross pens are recognized throughout the world as superior writing instruments.

What Is a Crusade?

A crusade is, simply put, something that's bigger than you are. It's a "cause" with an impact that reaches beyond your personal wants and needs.

Crusades can take all kinds of forms. They may be small or large. It doesn't matter what it is, as long as it's honest and decent. Don't let the earlier examples mislead you. Those were examples of business people whose crusade led to wealth. And often it works that way. People who are committed to a crusade and give it 110 percent are often rewarded financially. But a crusade may not have anything to do with making money; some of the most selfless crusades have had the most dramatic impact on the quality of life in America and the world.

Here are some crusaders who probably wouldn't be considered successes if you measured their worth in dollars. It's doubtful that they even thought about being successful. They never got rich, but think about the difference they made with their lives because they had a crusade.

On a trip to Africa, Dr. Albert Schweitzer fell in love with that land and its people. He couldn't bear the terrible need for medical help, and he began a one-man crusade to improve the health conditions and the lives of those people. His work won him a Nobel Peace Prize in 1952.

A middle-aged woman in Montgomery, Alabama, one day decided that having to give up her seat on the bus—just because she was black—was unfair, and she took a stand for the equality of all people. Rosa Parks's stand for human rights set off a movement that changed the course of history.

In India a small, frail man named Gandhi joined other countrymen to oppose the rule of the British. But refusing to engage in brutal battles where many would die, Gandhi proposed resistance through nonviolent means. At first, everyone laughed at him. Defeat the British Empire without firing a shot? But his followers—and the world—saw the strength of spirit in the man who refused to turn to violence. Gandhi's campaign for nonviolent change won freedom for his country and impacted the world.

While the rest of the world was focused on newer and better technology, Rachel Carson became concerned about the effects of progress on the natural resources of America. At first, everyone thought she was just an alarmist; but gradually, over a period of years, more people began to take notice. Finally her book *The Silent Spring* woke up the nation and began the environmentalist movement in America.

Crusaders have a mentality that's the opposite of the small child. They have made a "commitment to a cause," and they see their job as doing whatever they can to promote that cause. A crusade could be anything, in any area, but each one is unique because the individuals involved are committed to something that has far-reaching effects beyond them and their lives.

UNWRITTEN LAW:	*Crusaders commit to something bigger than their business.*

Crusaders Stand for Something

In the dog-eat-dog world of business, a lot of people think that the old moral values and principles just don't apply anymore. They think that the Christian principles taught in the Bible are stale and outdated. But crusaders stand for something. They know that how you live and how you conduct your business are more important than the bottom line. They believe that honesty and integrity are priorities, and they recognize that no cause is worth crusading for if it isn't built on a basis of goodness and rightness.

In my business, I try to look for the crusaders. But sometimes individuals come on board, and I can tell that they are lukewarm about the company's crusade for consumers. They're just in it to see if they can make a buck. Their attitude is, "Well, this is as good as anything else for making a living. This will help me pay the mortgage and give the kids lunch money."

That's not good enough if you want to do something special with your life. If you want to do something big, you've got to be part of something you are excited about and you believe in, something worthwhile. You've got to feel proud of what you're doing.

Again, I think of Coach Bear Bryant. What a great American! I think he was the best football coach who ever lived. If you want to be inspired, read his book called *The Bear.* A few years ago, I had a chance to meet him and spend the day with him. That guy was one tough, committed dude. He had taken a passion for football and turned it into his crusade. He believed in the power of the game to build people. He took pretty good high-school football players and taught them about discipline and commitment and pride. He taught them about how to win honorably and lose graciously. He taught a lot more than how to pass and tackle, that's for sure.

If you talked to him and his assistant coaches and the players, you quickly figured out that football to Coach Bryant was not some little deal where eleven folks play eleven folks and who cares if you win or not? To him, football was a way of life. That was the thing he chose to devote his life to.

Are You Afraid to Take a Stand?

So many people in America today are afraid to take a stand. They won't speak up for what they believe. Usually, it's because they can't stand the heat of opposition.

UNWRITTEN LAW:	*What's popular isn't always right, and what's right isn't always popular.*

We all want other people to like us. We all want to be popular. But taking a stand for what's right is the only way to be really proud of what we do. The other choice is doing what's wrong, and that's not likely to bring us any happiness or fulfillment. It's a lot better to be alone than to be in a crowd of people with low standards and values who will drag us down to their level. Steve Bartkowski, the NFL quarterback, is quoted as saying, "If you don't stand for something, you'll fall for anything." It's true. Having convictions and believing in something bigger than ourselves are protections against all the "thrills" that tempt

My parents, Arthur and Betty Williams. I didn't come from a privileged background. My daddy was a high school football coach and my mamma was a homemaker. They were "the greatest"!

Me at four years old. My dreams as a child were like those of most little boys . . . I wanted to be a star football player.

My wife to be . . .
Angela Jean Hancock.

I fell in love with Angela in the second grade.

Our high school days. Angela was a majorette and I played basketball and football. We lived for those games on Friday nights!

I quarterbacked for our team until I broke my arm my senior year. I was devastated, but it taught me that opportunities in life are not endless, and you must do all you can do each day to improve your life.

Five generations of my mother's family not long after my son was born. I'm now the oldest in my family. This picture symbolizes what I realized as I became a man—we're only here for a flicker.

One of my major concerns has always been the welfare of my family. I became committed to the term insurance philosophy when I found out I could get $100,000 of life insurance for the same price I was paying for a $15,000 policy.

Of all the people I have known, my only two heroes in life are Tommy Taylor and West Thomas, my high school coaches. Each man was like a daddy to me.

Charging the sidelines on Friday nights!

Our 1969 championship team.

It was an honor to receive "Coach of the Year" awards two out of the five years I was a head coach.

Rudy Allen and me. (See story in Chapter 2.)

Boe Adams, the "mastermind" and "genius" behind the A.L. Williams company.

Trudy White was the first and only home office employee when we set up shop in 1977 in a bare office north of Atlanta. She was the secretary, bookkeeper, receptionist, and office manager all rolled into one!

My longtime friend Bob Buisson. In addition to being my first full-time recruit, Bob was the first person in our company to be paid $100,000 in one year.

"I want Pru bad" was the battle cry of our company in 1983. We were only six years old. That dream came true the next year, as our people sold a total of $38 billion in individual life insurance, more than industry giant Prudential.

Like all new ideas, ALW stirred controversy in the beginning. But when we were featured as the cover story in *The Saturday Evening Post* in 1983, we knew we had "arrived."

Our company has had incredible success in only 10 short years. Thousands and thousands of people are turned on by our big dreams and positive way of thinking!

In 1984, after only seven short years in business, we achieved our biggest goal. We became No. 1 in total face amount of individual life insurance issued.

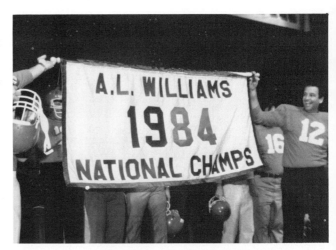

In 1986, A. L. Williams built the largest private, corporate satellite network in the world. This powerful education and communication tool is unique within the financial services industry.

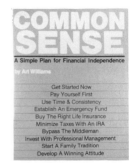

A.L. Williams is known as the "Common Sense Company." This book explains the simple financial principles on which our company was founded. Since its first publication in 1983, it has sold over 13 million copies.

Most companies have a boardroom; at our company, we call it the "War Room." Our competitive edge is one of our keys to winning!

To meet the needs of the largest sales force in the financial services industry, A. L. Williams had to establish its own printing company. Today, Greater Atlanta Printing has become one of the largest paper purchasers and in-house printing contractors in the Southeast.

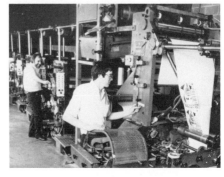

We started with one office and one employee in 1977. Today, the ALW Home Office Headquarters, located in an Atlanta suburb, is a massive complex with thousands of employees supporting a sales force of over 180,000.

Several of our company trips have been to Vienna, Austria, where we hold a fabulous ball. Not bad for a bunch of former teachers, coaches, and policemen!

Bagpiping in Scotland on one of our "Super Trips"!

From our "Rhine River" trip album in 1985.

Praise is one of the secrets to motivating people. No matter what your background, in this company you are SOMEBODY!

Learning the hula in Maui, Hawaii, another of our company's favorite vacation spots!

Dressed for the ball! We believe in a commitment to family, and the spouses of our leaders are welcome in every facet of the business — including our fabulous incentive trips!

"Bullet Bob" Turley. The best salesm[an] ever knew and a legend today in A.L. Williams.

Virginia Carter, one of our original seven vice presidents and the "First Lady" in our hearts.

Rusty Crossland, also one of our original vice presidents, and his family saw their dreams come to life.

We give plaques the size of doors in our company to encourage people to "dream big!" Hubert Humphrey was a railroad engineer before he joined A.L. Williams. He dreamed "big" and became the first person in our company to be paid $100,000 in one month.

It was an honor to receive Southern Illinois University's "Entrepreneur of the Year" award in 1987. This award was a result of the tremendous success of the ALW company.

One of the awards I cherish the most is the "Christian Business Leader of the Year" from the Christian World Affairs Conference in 1986. I credit my wife Angela with helping me to keep my priorities straight. My success would be meaningless without my faith in God and my love for my family.

My "mastermind group." Presidents have their "cabinets"; at our company, we have an "Inner Circle." Winning in business means selecting key leaders and rewarding them with special recognition for their effort.

Welcoming the President of the
United States, Ronald Reagan, to
Atlanta in 1986. It's hard to believe
that a former high school coach
finally made the "Big Leagues"!

Meeting with investment guru John Templeton,
of the world renowned Templeton mutual funds.
Investing for the future is an important part of the
A. L. Williams philosophy.

Angela and I with life insurance authority Arthur Milton. Milton is one of the many consumerists who support our company's simple philosophy of buying insurance strictly for death protection, not as an investment.

Meeting Vice President George Bush in 1986.

In the studio of ALW-TV with Gerry Tsai, CEO of Primerica Corporation. Gerry saw immediately the power of the dynamic ALW sales force.

Angela and I with our good friend Jerry Falwell.

Presenting Stanley Beyer, CEO of PennCorp Financial, with a "Wall of Fame" portrait. The commitment from Stanley's company to underwrite our term life insurance business in 1980 gave us the freedom to grow like never before.

Senior National Sales Director Ronnie Barnes epitomizes our company's belief in "dreaming big." A former school teacher from a small town, Ronnie today enjoys financial success he once never thought possible. A beautiful home in Tennessee and a private jet are just some of the rewards.

I believe one of the main reasons our company is winning is our "crusade." One of our representatives in California replaced Mr. Domingo Vigil's $20,000 whole life policy with a term policy that gave his family $200,000 of coverage. Thanks to our efforts, his family has been secure financially despite his death over a year ago.

us every day with false promises of wealth and excitement.

Some media people have called me "the most hated man in the insurance industry today." Naturally, I don't like to hear that, and my wife doesn't, either. But I have a crusade to offer American consumers a better way of handling the protection and investment needs of their families. If that makes me unpopular with other people in my industry, well, that's too bad. But that's not going to make me quit and go home.

You see, crusaders are often controversial. When you become a crusader, get ready. I learned in coaching and playing football that the team in the "wrong-colored" jersey is going to try to knock your head off. But look at the other side. The only way *not* to be controversial is to be average and ordinary. Call me anything but average and ordinary!

The Birth of a Crusade

When I was a football coach, I was a crusader. I wanted those kids to become great football players and become a unified team with confidence and style. I wanted that so bad I couldn't stand it. I'm convinced that made a big difference in my coaching.

But my coaching crusade can't really compare to the crusade that changed my life.

My dad was a special guy. He was a football coach, too, and I guess that's what gave me the love of the game that I still have today. He was a graduate of Vanderbilt University and got his master's degree in chemistry from Michigan State. Eventually, he left coaching and went to work at a pickle company in Cairo, Georgia. After working twenty years, my dad dropped dead one day of a heart attack. He was forty-eight. Like most people, my dad had been paying money to an insurance company for his entire adult life. A friend from our neighborhood had sold him his policies. Since most people aren't insurance experts, they rely on a trusted agent to sell them what's best for their families. That's what my dad did. He thought he was protecting us in case something unexpected happened. He had never accumulated much money, like most people in middle America, but he faithfully paid his insurance premium.

I was in college when he died, and my two younger brothers were in the sixth and tenth grades. Like most women of that era, my mother had never worked outside the home.

When that "something unexpected" did happen, we were devastated. The pain of losing our dad and my mother her husband was bad enough; but the next devastation came when we discovered that the insurance premium my father had struggled to pay for twenty years had not bought enough insurance to replace his income.

For the next several years, I tried to help support my own family and help take care of my mother and two brothers. I was in school and then a high-school coach, so my salary wasn't a lot of help. Those years were tough ones in a lot of ways, but I'll tell you, the toughest part by far was seeing my mother suffer the way she did.

Many years later, at a family reunion, something happened that stunned me. My cousin, who was an accountant, told me about the best kind of life insurance to own. At the time, I had a $15,000 policy of the type that's usually called "whole life" insurance. I wanted more, but that's all an average person like a football coach could afford. I knew it wasn't enough, but I didn't think there was any alternative.

Well, to make a long story short, my cousin introduced me to the concept of "buy term and invest the difference." He explained that whole life insurance combined death protection with a "forced" savings plan that paid a low rate of interest. This bundled product was much more expensive than the cost of pure death protection (term insurance). Plus, the amount saved between the cost of term and whole life could be placed in a high-return savings vehicle and produce many more savings dollars for retirement. He showed me how I could buy $100,000 of low-cost term insurance for the same premium I was paying for $15,000 of whole life.

I didn't believe him. If this was true, why didn't all the companies do it and advertise it? He explained that most companies had term, but because they didn't make as much profit from it, they made sure that agents received higher compensation for selling the more expensive product.

At first, I refused to believe that was true. I couldn't comprehend that an agent would go to a family he knew and sell them an expensive product that prevented them from buying enough insurance to protect their families, that would put them in my mother's position if a death occurred.

That next week, I was tormented by all I had heard. I went to the library and read everything I could get my hands on about insurance. And I found out that my cousin was telling the truth. All the experts said term insurance was the way to go. They said that most insurance agents owned term on their own lives, but they sold the more expensive product to others.

On that day, I became a crusader. All I could think of was how Angela, Art, and April would have suffered if I had died and they had been forced to live on my little $15,000 policy. Almost as upsetting was the knowledge that the insurance agent could have sold me $100,000 of term coverage for the same price. I got mad, and I'm still mad!

The more I read and studied and talked to people, the madder I got. It was true that almost all agents could sell their clients a term product if they wanted to, but they wouldn't get as much commission as they got from the sales of more expensive whole life products.

Don't get me wrong. I'm not saying that all agents are bad people. I realized that those companies with the famous names and the big buildings downtown put pressure on the agents to sell the high-priced products instead of the ones that people could afford. I guess those people didn't ever have to see the widows and children face-to-face, so they just tried not to think about them.

As it turned out, that talk with my cousin was a turning point in my life. I went from being a good football coach to a crusader for term insurance.

Educating consumers like myself about term insurance and investments became my crusade. Every time I thought of Angela and the kids and what could have happened to them, I just wanted to explode. But instead of exploding, I went to see three or four more people to tell them about my discovery. That's the difference between a "job" and a crusade.

I found my crusade in a place where I never expected to find it. I guess you could say I found it by accident.

But let me tell you this, folks—once you find your crusade, you'll never be the same again. I can testify that a crusade is a totally different thing from a job. Of course, you still work, and instead of working less, you work harder than you've ever worked in your life. The difference is that you don't mind. You've got a cause that's bigger than you are. You're committed to something more than yourself or your business. Whenever I was discouraged—and that was about a million times because the actual selling came very hard for me—I'd pass some young couple on the street and wonder what kind of insurance they had and if they were protected if something happened to one of them. And off I'd go again.

For a few years, I worked for other companies. But in each one, I didn't like the "corporateness" of it. My crusade was "buy term and invest the difference," but my dream was to reach financial independence for my family. At other companies, they appreciated good salesmen, but there was no chance to move up. Whenever a phenomenal salesman came along who was making tons of sales, pretty soon he'd be making as much as the president, and they'd cut his territory and push him back down somehow. I couldn't stand that, so I decided to form A. L. Williams.

Crusading in the Tough Times

Let me tell you, the first few years of my company were the roughest I've ever encountered. I don't wish them for anybody, and I hope I don't ever have to live through anything like them again.

I was so naive about corporate America. I didn't realize that some insurance companies didn't really want people to know about term insurance. They saw the buy-term-and-invest concept as a threat to their business. From the very beginning, we had problems. On one side, here's Art Williams and a few people who came with him from his former company, and here's these giant companies with whole rooms full of lawyers and lobbyists and executives on the other side.

It wasn't always a fair fight, and sometimes it could get pretty rough. Every time we tried to open up an office in a new place, the competition made it just as tough as they possibly could. They'd use every financial and political resource they had. They'd write horrible articles in the newspaper that humiliated my wife and kids. Those were tough times.

We weren't a bunch of experienced management executives. There were eighty-five of us starting out, and very few of us had an advanced degree or a lot of business experience. We had few administrative skills, no financial backing, no contract with a company, and a management team made up of ex-teachers and coaches and the like. (I guess that's why those guys who study companies for books like *In Search of Excellence* never came to study us!)

But you know what? We didn't quit. And you know why we didn't quit? Because it wasn't just a job. It was our life. It was the thing that made us get out of bed in the morning and not want to go to bed at night. We knew that what we were doing was right, and that's really all we needed. Every time we delivered a death claim to a widow for $100,000 or $200,000 instead of $10,000 or $15,000, we got a feeling that would take us through all the bad times.

To this day, I believe the reason for our company's success is not only the rightness of the product we sell. It's the crusading spirit that's evident everywhere from the mail room to the boardroom.

We all had our personal dreams, and most important, we had a crusade. And we made it.

How Do You Get a Crusade?

You're probably saying, "Well, Art, all that's fine, but I'm just a schoolteacher (or a fireman or a construction worker). Where is the crusade in my business?"

Wherever you find yourself in your life, there's room for a crusade. As you can see, my crusade started because of something that happened in my family. Many people are like A. T. Cross, and they have a crusade of doing something better than it's ever been done before, of producing something that makes people's lives easier or more enjoyable. A family in Ohio wanted to make the best jelly anywhere. That was their crusade. Today, people who love jelly won't buy any that doesn't come with a Smucker's label.

There's a crusade wherever you are. There was a young man who had a serious weight problem in high school. As an adult, he weighed 268 pounds. He was successful as a model (he was the guy in the grapes on those funny Fruit of the Loom commercials). But he didn't feel good about himself. One day he went out to his car and found a note: "Fat people die young. Please don't die. An Admirer." That's what it took to get him started.

He starved and crash dieted and lost nearly one hundred pounds in three months. He wrecked his body with his dramatic program, becoming dehydrated, losing his hair, and having all sorts of other health problems. Finally, he was hospitalized.

As he started over and began to learn how to lose weight safely through nutrition and exercise, he wanted to share his knowledge with other people like himself who were troubled by their weight problems. He was so excited and enthusiastic about helping people to solve a problem with which he identified (I do, too!) that people were attracted to him immediately. Eventually, he made weight loss education his business.

Today, Richard Simmons is recognized all over America for his weight loss crusade, and he has become wealthy and famous in the process.

No matter where you are in life or what your business is,

there's a crusade waiting to happen. Look around you, and get ready to make a difference.

But I'm Just ONE Person!

This brings me to another objection most people raise when I talk to them about having a crusade. They say, "Art, I'm just one person. What can *one person* do that could possibly make a difference in this huge world of ours?" Or "Art, I'm just an ordinary person. People like me can't be involved in big movements."

What about some of the people I've mentioned like Gandhi and Albert Schweitzer? All were "just one person" with no particular visions of greatness. But their dedication to a crusade was responsible for dramatic changes in our world.

In a town in California, a young housewife and mother was devastated by the death of her thirteen-year-old daughter who was killed in a car accident. The driver of the other vehicle was drunk and had a record of previous drunk driving arrests.

Feeling the heartbreak of her own situation, and the heartbreak of so many other mothers who had shared a similar situation, she decided to take action. She simply refused to sit back and do nothing. She organized a group of mothers in her area, with the goal of getting the drunk drivers off the road by making them accountable for the victim's death. The mothers held their first press conference in Sacramento on August 26, 1980, calling on the governor to create a state task force to study the problem of drunk driving.

The mothers then took their concerns to courts, to district attorneys, to the police, and to offices of traffic safety. Everywhere they went, they were told the same thing. "Give up. This is an insurmountable problem, and you'll never get anywhere." There were a lot of obstacles. Drunk driving was a volatile issue; many people were guilty of doing it, sometimes even the lawmakers themselves. Over and over the group was told to "forget it."

Just think about it. This wasn't a group of influential people or legislators or lawmakers. We're talking about *housewives,* a group that, often unfairly, has been perceived as powerless. Everywhere they went they got the message: "How can a bunch of housewives expect to change the system?"

But the group grew, literally mother by mother, woman by woman. The press lost interest, but the women went back to the traffic safety departments and the courts to plead for action. They spoke to school and community groups, anyone who would listen. They conducted workshops to raise awareness of the problem. They taught themselves how to lobby—maybe not in a "professional" way, but from the heart. Finally, they reached an assemblywoman in the state legislature who introduced a bill. Slowly, people began to take them seriously.

Eventually, the entire country was awakened to the seriousness of the problem, and the Mothers Against Drunk Driving (MADD) began to make their mark. Today, there are 950 new anti–drunk driving laws on the books. There are over four hundred chapters of MADD in the U.S. and chapters in Great Britain, Canada, Sweden, and New Zealand, boasting over half a million members.

Since MADD had the courage to take a stand, one by one, others have jumped on the bandwagon. Several years ago, you saw the first TV ads cautioning people, "Don't drive drunk." Then taxi services and bars began advertising that they would pay your fare home on New Year's Eve. Recently, even the alcohol industry has taken the cue, urging people not to drink and drive. This type of awareness and effort never existed before MADD came onto the scene.

They were just a group of "ordinary" housewives and mothers; but their work has changed the thinking in this country about driving "under the influence"—and saved perhaps millions of lives and a lot of heartbreak.

Learning to Reach Higher

We've all heard the saying, "A man's reach should exceed his grasp." It's true, and that's one of the best "side effects" of having a crusade.

A crusade motivates you and others to reach higher and farther. A crusade does more than anything else to motivate people and to bring excitement to the day-to-day grind. A crusade makes you get out of bed in the morning when you want to sleep. People need a purpose; they want to commit to something bigger than a business; they want to make the world a better place to live. They can't get that kind of satisfaction in most organizations; the only payoff employees usually see for all their efforts is that the company makes more money. People want to do something good for others, and that makes all the difference in their commitment.

Once you've become a crusader, you'll recognize other crusaders. And if you're like me, you'll start looking for them. As president of a company now, I know it makes a big difference. Give me a crusader any day, somebody who wants to be the best, who's got a dream and wants to be a part of our crusade. By looking for people with those two elements, I think we've put together one of the most amazing companies in modern business history.

I don't care about a person's background; I don't care about problems in the past. If a person's a dreamer and a crusader, I want him or her on my team. If I see somebody, no matter what the job, who is pushing to be the best at that job—being a front desk receptionist or a mail clerk or a printer—and the person is going at that job 110 percent, then that's who I want to promote. I don't care if those people don't have an M.B.A. or fifteen years of experience. If they love the crusade and want to be somebody special and do something special with their lives, that's all I need to know. You can take your employment tests and psychological profiles and all that stuff and toss it over a bridge.

I've been fortunate enough to learn this lesson by watching some incredible people. I know it's true. Our company didn't get where it is today, after ten short years, by taking things easy. I've seen people here work like I've never seen people work anyplace else I've been. A couple of times a year, we have conventions for our salespeople. We try to make them a combination of learning and enjoyment, and we have them in beautiful locations. At one meeting in New Orleans in 1987, we had twelve thousand people. You'd think it would take hundreds of people to run that large a meeting. In fact, most companies hire outside firms to handle such massive jobs. We don't. We do it all in-house with our own people.

I've seen people work nights, weekends, around the clock, days and weeks without a day off. Well, any of you out there who manage people know that you can't make people work like that. If I came in and said, "Everybody here has to work twenty straight days with no breaks," not only would I be sued, I'd probably be hung out on a rail. I don't tell those people to work like that. At any time, they can come and tell me that something we'd like to do is impossible. And sometimes they have to do that. But these people will work days and nights and weekends, usually without me even knowing about it till later. They'll work a ten-day convention with two or three hours of sleep per night. Their salaries are good, but I could never pay them enough to make that kind of effort worth it. And I'm not talking about just executives, who make the highest salaries. I'm talking about the guys who run the presses at our printing operation, the artists who design the materials, the distribution workers who box it all up for transport, the travel people who work night and day to make sure the travel arrangements for twelve thousand people go off without a hitch.

These people have lives and families and children, and they'd rather be home. But when the situation calls for it, they'll nearly kill themselves to get everything done—and done right. No leader or manager could ever force people to work like that. They'd all quit and get another job. But I've seen people do miraculous things, time and time again, because they believed in what they were doing.

It's unbelievable. I've been shown over and over and over again what people can do when they believe in something, when they feel like they're a part of something bigger than themselves. When people feel like they're doing something to help other people, something that's got meaning, their lives have a new purpose. I've seen it for years, and I'm still amazed, but I know in my heart that it's true.

Some people talk about finding out what they were born to do. I do think there are people who seem to know from Day One what their mission in life is. But that's not true for all of us. I know I didn't ever dream that my crusade would be life insurance. Most of us need to look around and find something to believe strongly in, something that moves us and we feel good about. If you find something to believe in and it offers you fulfillment of your dreams, you're home free. Don't get me wrong. I didn't say it was going to be easy. I just said it was going to be worth it.

Create a purpose in life for yourself. Commit to something bigger than your personal desires. It doesn't have to be something that makes you a millionaire. And it doesn't have to be what somebody else thinks would be a good purpose for you. Be yourself—hold on to your dream—and find a cause worth fighting for.

CHAPTER SEVEN

Dream Big— But Keep It Simple

Genius is the ability to reduce the complicated to the simple.

C. W. Cerar

I'm not sure who Cerar is, but he sounds like one more smart dude, I'll tell you that.

A big mistake that people make when they fail in business or even at life is trying to complicate things. It seems to be human nature for people to believe that something is "better" when it's difficult or complicated.

I can certainly understand how people fall into this trap. So much in modern technology has revolutionized this century that it seems people can't help idolizing the complicated. Seventy years ago, we were awed by telephones. Twenty years later, we were awed by television. Thirty years after that, we were awed by space travel. Today, we have computers, microwave ovens, answering machines, car phones . . . you name it. With all our incredible technology, we've developed a definite lack of respect in this country for the "simple." We think that the more complicated something is, the more valuable it is. We've come to associate what is complex with what will work.

Wrong. Wrong. Wrong.

Complicated may work for machines, but it doesn't work for people. You can't let all the high-tech part of our society influence you and the way you run your life or your business. *You've got to keep it simple.*

Several years ago, a young Harvard law and business graduate decided to start his own business. With the help of his grandfather, a successful Wall Street investor, he thought he would build his own beverage company. After a couple of weeks in the business, the two men met for lunch. The grandfather asked the graduate how many customers he had. The grandson replied, "None yet. I've been very busy hunting the proper computer system." "Son, until you have customers, you don't need a computer system. You don't even need an office or a desk. You need customers." Listening to the advice of his successful mentor, the graduate put aside the lessons in "strategic planning" he'd learned in college and went out in search of customers. Today, his business is a true American success story. His beverages are sold across the nation. To this day, he has no office or desk. When asked why, he replies, "Because you can't sell anything to a desk."

What a fabulous lesson in business! Don't let your respect for modern technology replace the fundamentals of what will make your business a success. Focus on what generates income, and put your time and effort in this area.

Three Keys to Keeping It Simple

If you want to see your business take off, follow these simple steps:

1. *Manage activity.*

To be a success in business, you've got to take action. You can't sit in a chair all day, trying to analyze what's wrong with your business. You'll never generate any income.

One of my favorite stories that I tell to people in our company is about an insurance company in Chicago that called in a marketing consulting firm to analyze what was wrong with their business. The company was averaging only two and a half sales per agent per month. They had tried everything they knew to get that company moving, and after two years, they still had a low average. When the sales expert came in and looked at the situation, he replied, "Your number-one problem is that you just aren't seeing enough people."

It was too simple for the company to accept. To prove his point, the sales expert asked to see twenty salespeople. They would have to be a cross section ranging from the best to the worst salesmen. When they were selected, the expert told his sales force, "Here's your whole presentation. When you go out and talk to a prospect, I don't want you to say anything but this one statement: 'You don't want any life insurance, do you?'"

That was it, just that one negative message. And the salesmen were to see how many people they could repeat that message to.

So each one set out to talk to people and say, "You don't want any life insurance, do you?"

Nearly all of the people responded, "You're right. Get lost."

But one out of every sixty people responded, "Hallelujah. Great. Come in. I've been looking for you all my life. Sign me up."

And since each salesman found that he could repeat that message to about sixty people a day, he averaged one sale a day. The company's business took off, and it was saved.

Activity is the key, and I'm not talking just about the "sales" business. In *any* business, you have to take *action*.

2. *Create little successes.*

Sometimes, when you look at a business goal, it can seem so overwhelming that you want to give up before you've even tried. A trick I learned was to break down the goal into more bite-size parts. If my goal was to save $1,000 a month, I needed to make at least four sales. That was pretty intimidating. To get four sales, I'd probably have to make eight or ten presentations. To make eight or ten presentations, I'd need twice as many prospects because a lot of people wouldn't even make an appointment. Four sales started to sound impossible! The only way to deal with that was to break it down into little pieces. If I could manage to get one prospect a day and make just two presentations a week, I could make my four sales a month. Anybody could do that. This technique gave me little successes along the way, which kept me motivated.

Even if you do only one positive thing a day, your confidence gets a real boost, and you eliminate some of the fear of failure lurking in the back of your mind.

3. *Don't get bogged down in paperwork.*

It was a critical point during World War II. General MacArthur and his troops were camped at the side of a big river, and they had to get across. MacArthur called in his engineer and said, "Soldier, how long will it take you to throw a bridge across that river?" The engineer replied, "Three days." MacArthur said, "Good, have your draftsman draw up plans immediately." Three days later, MacArthur called the engineer back into his office to ask how the bridge was coming along. "Sir," replied the engineer, "the bridge is finished, and you can take your troops across now provided you don't have to wait for the plans. They're not done yet."

Nothing will get you into more trouble in your business life than if you take your eye off the ball. In this case, the "ball" means your ultimate goal, whether it's to build a bridge across a river or to build the city's largest ice-cream stand.

Like the Harvard graduate I talked about earlier, it's so easy to get sidetracked. And paperwork can be a real killer, especially in the tough times when you really don't want to go out there and do the plain old hard work that's necessary to win.

In my business, many men and women spend so much time processing the applications and filling out home office forms that they don't have time to make any sales. One of the first things I did when I started my business was to get some good administrative help so I wouldn't be bogged down in paperwork. I don't believe in a good leader doing administrative work because that leaves no time to see customers or clients.

Recently, I was with one of our newest and hottest young vice presidents, David Hyles. David was making really good money. After being in the business only twelve months, he'd won our sales reward trip to Vienna and Paris. He was telling me (proudly) how he had a big business, but no secretary in his office. I said, "David, that's a mistake. You're trying to save money in the wrong area. Your time is worth $300 to $400 an hour. Get someone else to do your administrative work."

David went home and did just that. I called him several weeks later to ask how things were going. "Art," he said, "things are unbelievable. We've got a secretary, and I'll bet my business is up at least 25 percent."

Have a Simple Business Game Plan

Earlier, while you were reading about the Harvard graduate who started his own company, did you catch yourself wondering what "strategic planning" was? Do you worry that you'll be "behind the game" by not coming up with long-range planning? You need to plan. That's critical. But you increase your chances of winning when you simplify that plan.

I read a story recently about a young executive from a small town outside Atlanta. At twenty-eight, he found himself in charge of an ailing family business, a textile mill. When the young man first took over the business, the problems seemed insurmountable—lack of financing for tremendous debt, antiquated equipment, endless meetings between middle management that seemed to get nowhere. After finding a good corporate sponsor and setting up a purchasing program to update the plant's equipment, the young executive turned to his problems in-house. He moved the decision-making process to the lowest level, eliminating much of the middle management. Purchases, in the millions of dollars, were made by department heads who dealt with the problems on a daily basis and had firsthand knowledge of the business. No meetings. No memos. Just the right people making decisions about their work. Simplicity earned the company sales in the hundreds of millions of dollars that year.

I became convinced of the value of a simple game plan when I got my first head coaching job. I had been preparing all my life to be a head football coach. Throughout high school and college, every step I took was to reach that goal. When I got my first assistant coaching job, I was still preparing. I'd go to coaching clinics and carefully take notes. I accumulated piles and piles of information and studied like you wouldn't believe. The result was the most beautiful playbook you've ever seen. It was the playbook of my dreams. There must have been fifty different running plays and thirty different passing plays. It was fifty pages thick.

When I finally got my break as a head coach, I was so excited. I was in charge. *I* was going to be the one to make the call on fourth down with one minute left in the game. I had a lot of confidence, and with all my studies and my beautiful playbook, I just knew I could produce a winning team.

When spring practice rolled around, I saw what I was up against with my team. It was the team I talked about earlier— the one with players who didn't even know how to get down in a stance or hold the football. They were so unskilled that we had to start from scratch just practicing fundamentals. I threw away my playbook. I wound up using about six basic plays. When I left two years later to take another head coaching job at a bigger high school, my playbook was only ten pages thick. I still had only six basic plays in my playbook, and with those plays I built a championship program at the new school.

I've learned to simplify every plan I come up with, whether it's my personal savings program or a business decision. One of the best examples is a prospecting tool we developed. When our company got big enough to think about marketing tools (and it was five years before we felt comfortable enough to add "extras"), I wanted to put together a financial handbook that people could understand.

You see, year after year, it seemed that everyone we came in contact with through our business had trouble managing finances. While I was a coach making $10,700 a year, Angela and I saved $42,000 over a two-and-a-half-year period by my coaching and working part-time in insurance and investments. So I knew it wasn't because understanding finances was only for "smart" people. It was because Angela and I knew what we had to do to be able to save that kind of money.

A lot of books were out there on the market about how to organize a budget, how to save for retirement, and so on, but almost all of them were in small print, overflowing with complicated words and concepts. And most of them were long and tedious to read. It's no wonder the average consumer's personal financial situation is a mess.

I dreamed of a book that would include valuable information, but would be set in a format that people like me could relate to. I had a crystal clear picture in my mind of what we needed. I wanted large print, short chapters, big pictures and graphs, like you find in magazines, and I wanted it to be written with simple, short sentences. I got so excited about this book that I became obsessed with it. The publications people worked around the clock to get it out. I felt deep inside that we were really on to something.

Even the name of the book had to be just right. I came up with *Common Sense*. When my family heard that, they said, "Art, why do you want to call your book that? That title by itself doesn't make any sense." Maybe they were right. But it was simple, and I felt that people like me could relate to it.

We finished the book and guess what? We now have over fourteen million copies of *Common Sense* in print. *Common Sense* is available in Spanish and French editions as well as in English. It's been requested for use by financial institutions, CPA fraternal organizations, and federal government agencies. It's even been used as a text for economics, business, and insurance courses in colleges, vocational schools, and high schools. Now *that* should tell you something about the value of simplicity!

My crusade to keep it simple has spilled over into every

aspect of the ALW business. One of the things I'm the most proud of in our company is our philosophy of keeping our product simple. We believe in insurance as nothing more than death protection. We are totally against complicating the picture for the consumer by using life insurance as an investment, a tax shelter, collateral for a loan, or anything else that makes it difficult for the average person to understand what he's getting. We believe the consumer is better off when he keeps his investments separate.

Unlike most other companies, we have one main product, a term life insurance product. Now, I won't bore you with any information about life insurance because the point I'm trying to make is that we simplify things. Other companies have hundreds of products with rate books an inch thick. Our rate book is one page thick—because the best product we can possibly sell, we sell to everyone.

Maybe you're trying to make a decision about how many items to offer on your restaurant menu. Keep it simple. Or maybe you're trying to boost sales in your retail store. Keep it simple. Whatever your business is, look at it from the standpoint of how you can reduce something complicated down to something simple.

Be Brief

Have you ever met anyone who was afraid to write in simple language for fear others would think he was "dumb"? This is the person who is always looking up substitute words in a dictionary to try to give the letter a more sophisticated sound.

Dumb. Dumb. Dumb.

If the letter was grammatically correct and had a clear message, the person reading it wouldn't stop for a minute to wonder where all the impressive words were. All he'd remember is what the writer was trying to communicate, and that's what's important.

UNWRITTEN LAW: *The shorter your message, the greater the effect.*

Maybe it's my own personal philosophy, but I'm famous for writing short letters. About 98 percent of my letters are one paragraph with only three or four sentences. And instead of signing "Sincerely" or "Yours Truly," I always wind up with "GO-GO-GO!" I want everyone to get my message! The point is, don't be afraid to keep your message simple and to the point. I don't care who the audience is. It may be middle America, or it may be college professors. People respond to something that's easy to understand.

All of us could learn a lesson from advertising. I have a lot against advertisers because I believe they have a negative effect on our self-esteem by promoting unrealistic portrayals of life and people. But let's face it, television ads are a tremendous measure of what "works" with people. Let me list a few ads and see if you can remember their impact on you:

✔ WHERE'S THE BEEF?
✔ COKE IS IT
✔ WE TRY HARDER
✔ JUST SAY NO

These ads were a smash success because they had a powerfully short message.

If you had to pick one saying in our company—and we love slogans—by far the most popular and most effective has been the phrase "Do It." Nothing more, just "Do It." I talk more about this in another chapter, but I'm bringing it up here because the simplicity of that message is greater than any two-hour speech I could give. You'll see that message embroidered in needlepoint, framed and hanging on ALW office walls across the country. You'll see it printed on T-shirts, on bumper stickers, in newsletters. It's everywhere.

When I speak at meetings, I generally wear a shirt that has in great big letters "NSD." That stands for "National Sales Director," the next to highest position in our company. Three letters, and the message to all those people is clear—"Go for NSD."

What about products in our society? Some of the most revolutionary products have been the simplest. Where would we be without Post-it notes? Safety pins? Bic pens? Disposable razors? I could go on and on, but I hope you're getting my point. Don't ever underestimate the value of simplicity.

Simplify with the Human Touch

One of the toughest parts of a job in sales is calling on people. Salespeople will go to great lengths to avoid face-to-face contact with a prospect. Every day, when I first started this business, I had to make myself talk to one more person. I got nauseated just thinking about the icy looks I would get and the way people would say, "No!"

Jerry Byer, one of our national sales directors in Michigan, was no different from me. Jerry was as outgoing as they come, but if there was a way to avoid getting a "no" face-to-face, he would do it. At the time, some people were sending out prospecting postcards in an effort to generate new business. Jerry and his organization sent those things out by the hundreds and had some luck with them.

But I saw that the mailers were starting to hurt our image because people don't like to get junk mail. I made a rule to eliminate them. The new rule devastated Jerry, and his organization had to start over again, talking to people face-to-face about our company and our product. You know what? Jerry had an explosion of business like you wouldn't believe. He was suddenly getting twice the number of "yeses" that he had with the postcards, and his business exploded. Today, Jerry's business is cash flowing more than $500,000 a year, and the only way people in his organization prospect is by meeting people.

Rich Thawley, a national sales director with our company

in San Jose, California, has been one of our company's best re-
cruiters. He can find just the right people and take them and
train them into superstars. Rich has always been excited and
motivated and let our simple message of buy term and invest
the difference be the key to his recruiting efforts. About three
years ago, though, there was a wave of excitement in the field
about a referral system. In actuality, the "system" was nothing
more than just asking people if they knew of anyone who might
be interested in our company and what we were offering. But
Rich and his organization were so enamored by the system that
they decided to get fancy with it. Instead of just asking people
and then scribbling names on a piece of paper, they got the
idea of having special cards printed up for people to list refer-
rals. Well, as soon as he began to use the cards, Rich's recruiting
efforts dropped off. It seems that the sophisticated method had
nowhere near the effect on people as the simple, scribbled list of
names on a piece of paper. With the old way, clients saw excitement about our company; they saw a genuineness not present in
the fancy cards. Needless to say, Rich quit using the cards and
went back to the old-fashioned way.

Keep it simple, and use the human touch.

When I first started talking to people about term insurance,
I had nothing more with me than a calculator, a pen, and a legal
pad. I didn't have a fancy brochure to convince people, and I
didn't wear a coat and tie. I wore my coaching shorts many
times. It worked because *nothing got in the way of my message* to
people. They were able to focus on the most important thing—
how I could save them money.

Believe in YOU

Accepting yourself for who you are is an important part of
keeping it simple. You've got to believe in yourself and whatever characteristics God gave you. Don't try to change them to
suit other people. Where would I be if I had let the fact that I
was a coach stop me from learning about the insurance I had?
I could have said, "Well, I'll leave that to somebody who has

gone through a six-week training course with an insurance company." Folks, I took that six-week training course, and you know what I found out? I found that I had learned enough about life insurance to make an intelligent decision before I ever took that course.

Where would I be today if I was insecure about my background and who I am? I certainly wouldn't be traveling and speaking before thousands of people at seminars and investment bankers in Europe and meeting the president of the United States.

You've got to believe in yourself and your background. The minute you do, you'll see that people will accept you and appreciate you for who you are. The key is believing in yourself. If you don't believe in you, no one else will, either.

Don't be embarrassed to operate on a simplistic level. Stop being afraid that someone will discover you're not a "brain."

We have a dress code in our company that I'm proud of, and I think it carries a message about my philosophy of keeping it simple. Whether you're in the field or working at the home office, you don't have to dress "fancy." The men don't have to wear a coat and tie to work. Most people wear what I call casual dress clothes, but very few of our people in the field or the home office wear a suit. I keep a suit in the closet of my office to put on in "emergencies," when my staff feels that I absolutely cannot get away with wearing my sport shirt and slacks.

Now, I'm not telling you all this to try to get you bankers or investment people to join the fight for comfortable work clothes (although I doubt you can find one man on Wall Street who enjoys wearing a tie), but I am saying that we operate simply. Our company doesn't try to be something we're not. This type of belief in ourselves is one of the reasons we're number one.

Let me leave you with one final thought about believing in yourself. About three years ago, I was asked to speak before a group of financial planners in Atlanta. It was kind of a contradiction in terms for me because I believe that often people like financial planners have misled the American public into thinking that managing their money is a difficult thing to do. But some home office people convinced me that I should do it for "PR" reasons. So I got dressed up in a coat and tie and went to their monthly luncheon. I had been "coached" to "tone it down" before this group. Our home office people had warned me that these people would be looking to discredit me any way they could since I often preach against their high-finance philosophies. So the speech I had prepared was different from the normal message I deliver to people who are interested in our company.

I got up to the podium and looked out over a room full of people who were mainly occupied with eating. They were clanking dishes and talking to each other. About five minutes into my speech, they were still clanking dishes and talking to each other. No one was listening, which kind of got to me. So I made a decision. I took my notes and threw them down behind the podium. I started to talk in plain English. I started to talk to those financial planners the same way I talk to people who come to our seminars across the country. I gave them the same speech that I give when I know I'm talking to people like me—coaches, teachers, policemen, firemen—people I can relate to. And you know what?

Table by table, I saw faces turn toward me. I saw people lay down knives and forks and set down their glasses. People stopped talking. The room got so quiet, you could have heard a pin drop. I spoke that way for about thirty minutes, longer than most of the speakers they normally had, and at the end, they gave me a standing ovation.

Folks, those men and women weren't impressed because I'd come up with a speech just for their "type." They were bored with that speech. They were people, no different from me. They didn't just accept my simplicity, they loved it!

Stop and consider these points. Are you comfortable enough with you? Do you feel good enough about you that you can be yourself and not be taken in by something that looks complicated and sophisticated? Folks, this is critical. It takes a "big" person to cut through all the unnecessary baloney and

CHAPTER EIGHT

Always Be Positive

Positive thinking is the key to success in business, education, pro football, anything that you can mention. . . . I go out there thinking that I'm going to complete every pass.

Ron Jaworski
Former NFL quarterback

It's not for sale. You don't inherit it. Nobody else can give it to you. You can't go to college and get it.

But it is the chief weapon in your arsenal for combating society's failure messages and your own internal enemy.

It's a *positive winning attitude.*

Folks, the difference between being great and being average and ordinary is such a thin thing it's almost too scary to talk about. A positive winning attitude is one of those "little edges" that mean the difference between winning and losing.

UNWRITTEN LAW: *I believe you can do 99 percent of the things right but not possess a positive winning attitude, and you will fail.*

I believe that if you possess a winning attitude and learn to make it work for you in your business and your life, you'll win. I'll go even further. I believe a positive winning attitude is the difference between being good and being great.

Before Things Can Change, You Must Change

I can clearly remember the events that led up to the longest day of my life. I was an assistant coach at Thomasville, a great football school in Georgia. Nobody loved coaching more than I did. But I wanted to be a head coach so bad I couldn't stand it. So I interviewed with a number of schools and finally got an offer. My head coach in high school, who was like a second daddy to me, had coached at the same school twenty years earlier.

Just a few days later, rumors began to circulate that the head coach at our school had had another offer, too. When this happened, the superintendent of Thomas County schools called me in and said, "Art, you have a great reputation around here, and if, in fact, our head coach leaves, we'd like for you to be the head coach at Thomasville. I hear you've had another job offer, and if you feel you have to take that one, I'll understand."

I couldn't believe it; I was really flattered.

Now, this was a school! It was one of the best in Georgia. It had a winning reputation. It had great facilities. The football team had *eight* full-time assistant coaches. It was a dream come true.

So I ran to talk to the head coach at Thomasville. He said, "Well, Art, I've had a couple of good offers, but I turned them down and decided to stay." I was disappointed, but since there wasn't going to be a job after all, I went ahead and signed the contract with the other school.

I went to the new school, and I worked like you can't believe. I knew this was my chance to prove myself. I talked to all the booster clubs. I talked to the student body. Seventy-seven kids came out for the team. I was pumped up.

Then things started to go wrong. At the end of the first week, fifty-four of those kids dropped out. We were down to just twenty-three kids. We didn't even have enough to scrimmage. I had only one assistant coach. We had poor facilities. Actually, we had poor *everything*.

I stood out on the sidelines at practice and looked at those kids. They were small and scrawny; they were weak; they didn't have any experience. They didn't even know the basic fundamentals of the game. Regardless of the names on their jerseys, when I looked out there, the only word I saw written on them was *loser.*

All of a sudden, the reality of the situation hit me in the face. I didn't know what I was going to do. I realized the whole situation was a disaster.

Three weeks into spring practice, the head coach at Thomasville resigned.

I was dumbfounded. I could have been *head coach* of one of the top football teams in Georgia. Instead, I was stuck in a "nothing" situation! I went home and wandered around in a state of shock for two days. The situation went around and around in my mind. *What have I done? Is somebody trying to destroy my life? Why am I being punished like this? There's no way for me to win with this crew I've got, and I could have had the best.* I honestly thought I would die.

Back then, most high schools had sort of an alumni game at the end of spring practice. You'd have the graduating seniors and some of the former players come back and play the new team. The past team had won only one game in two years. Worst football team you ever saw. So on Thursday before our first game on Friday, we just issued them uniforms. They didn't have a coach or anything; they didn't even practice.

I thought that even in our pitiful condition, we would beat them about 110–0. The town was on fire. Everybody in town came out to see the new coach and new team.

You guessed it. We were beaten by a bunch of guys who didn't even have a coach. I was in a state of shock. I've never been so humiliated in my life. I'll never forget that feeling.

Remember what I said earlier about failure messages? Man, that little enemy inside my head was working overtime. "Art, you're such a dud. I can't believe things could work out this bad for anyone. How could you be so stupid? Why didn't you wait and see what that coach was going to do? Why did you have to go jump into a bad situation? Nobody else would have done anything so stupid. Your football career is gettin' ready to end right here and now. You're through!"

That weekend, I went through the motions of living. I was totally convinced that Art Williams was a double-dumb dud.

I felt totally helpless. Life had dealt me a bad hand, and there was nothing I could do about it. I was trapped in the worst situation I could imagine—every coach's nightmare. All I could think about was the new coach at Thomasville, getting a great team and great equipment and great support. All the stuff that should have been *mine*.

Boy, what an attitude problem I had! I was feeling so sorry for myself and wallowing around in all those failure messages that I hadn't even stopped to think about anybody else. I blamed everything and everybody else for my situation. I assumed that I was stuck in it to the bitter end, and there was nothing I could do about it. I was the most unhappy person you'd ever find.

But you know something else? That "worst day of my life" turned out to be one of the best days. It sure didn't seem that way at the time, but looking back, I realize that what I learned from the experience changed my whole life.

I knew you ought to have a positive attitude about life, but those were just words to me. I thought it could help you out, but I didn't know it could change the way things turn out for you.

I don't know what opened my eyes and caused me to really look at the team. I guess in all that self-pity I suddenly realized I had a responsibility to them. I took a long look at myself, and it hit me. I said, "Art, what are you thinking about? You're a coach. When you told those kids that you were going to have a winning program, they believed you. They trusted you." I realized that I was going to coach a lot of kids in my life as the years went on, but these juniors and seniors would never have another chance to play football. They were depending on me to make their football days something special. And I was off somewhere holding my own "pity party."

A Change in Attitude

I made a decision, a conscious decision, to change my attitude—about that school, about that football program, and especially about that team. I decided that I was going to be a great football coach for them, even if I had to hide my heartbreak and disappointment.

I went back to school on Monday, and I started working. I started looking at those players as winners. We painted the dressing room; I bought new lockers; I did anything I could think of that would build a little pride in those kids. I praised every little thing they did right (and sometimes I had to look hard). I told them what great players they were going to be, how tough they were.

In the fall, we started preparing weeks before the other teams. We practiced the fundamentals over and over again. There weren't many of us, but we worked.

We won our first game, then our second, and we kept winning. Our fourth or fifth game was against the number-one team in the state, Waycross High School. I knew we couldn't win, but I just wanted those kids to go out there and compete.

But we did win, 14–7. Just a few months earlier, on that same football field, we had been beaten by those seniors with no coach who had won one game in two years. That night I was so ashamed of our team. But on this night our team had beaten the number-one team in the state of Georgia.

Those kids played their hearts out, and when they left that school, they had some special memories. I had a lot of other teams along the way, but that team will always be special. That year, I was voted Coach of the Year. That experience taught me one of the most valuable lessons of my life.

UNWRITTEN LAW: *For things to get better, you must get better.*

The players on that little football team were just as devastated as I was. They didn't see themselves winning anything. I wanted a great team, and they were a lousy team. I didn't think anything could change that, but *my* attitude did change it. As soon as I decided that it was going to be a great football year, it started to become a great football year. When I made a conscious decision to stop crying and start building a dream, it happened. Those kids wanted to believe they were special, but they needed somebody to believe in them.

When I changed my attitude about what I was doing, everything else changed. It works every time. I learned that nothing is going to change in your life unless you change. But if you're willing to change your attitude, you can start to change your life almost immediately.

Fundamentals of a Winning Attitude

There are four fundamentals of developing and maintaining a winning attitude: Always be excited, stop making excuses, always be "up," and make a total commitment.

Fundamental #1: *Always be excited.*

I hope you're starting to realize that there's no trick to winning. It's an everyday, all-the-time thing. More than anything else, it's an attitude. And more than 90 percent of having a positive attitude is being excited. It's easy to be excited when everything's going great. The tough thing is being excited when things aren't going so great—when you don't feel good or you've had a dispute with your spouse or your business looks like it's going down the tubes. But you've got to get excited and stay excited if you want to win. Your ability to deal with negatives or problems—to get them out of your system and go on—determines whether or not you'll be a success.

UNWRITTEN LAW: *More than 90 percent of winning is being excited.*

I'd even revise that unwritten law this way:

More than 90 percent of winning is being excited, *especially when you don't feel like being excited.*

A PERSONAL GOAL

One of my main goals is to go one twenty-four-hour day, just one, before they plant me in the ground and not have a single negative thought—no worries, no fears, nothing. I believe the most powerful people on the earth today are only positive for minutes at a time or hours at a time, maybe days at a time, in rare cases.

Every time I try to get on a positive kick, a couple of hours later something knocks me for a loop. I believe that it's your ability to muster up the courage, deep down inside, in spite of those worries and fears that will make you get up and go for it when others quit.

UNWRITTEN LAW: *Most people can stay excited for two or three months. A few people can stay excited for two or three years. But a winner will stay excited for twenty or thirty years—or as long as it takes to win.*

If you're a leader of other people, you've got to set an example of being excited.

UNWRITTEN LAW: *People won't follow a dull, disillusioned, frustrated crybaby.*

If you're excited, you draw people like a magnet. Everyone wants to know what you're feeling. They all want to experience the kind of excitement you have.

EXCITEMENT IS CONTAGIOUS

When I was working on my master's degree at Auburn University, I wrote my thesis on the motivation of the high-school athlete. I used an example given to me by an English teacher friend that I ate lunch with every day. Often she would say, "Art, I don't know what's happening to kids today. They don't pay attention in class. I can't get them to do fifteen minutes of homework. They don't even try!"

And I'd look at my football program. The kids had to volunteer to come out for football. It's not something that's required. They could be out flirting with a girlfriend, going to the movies, listening to music, or going to the beach, but they volunteered for my football team. When the bell would ring and all the other kids would go out and have fun, my boys would put on a uniform and that old helmet and go out on that football field where Coach Williams would be hollering at them and making them run wind sprints.

After football season when there were no names in the newspaper, no crowds in the stands, they would have to go down to the weight room and pump those weights for hours. I started thinking, *Why? Why can I get so much out of those kids when this English teacher can't get her kids to be excited for fifteen minutes about English?*

My conclusion was that it comes down to two things. First, motivation is everything, like I said earlier. Those kids were so motivated to be out there on Friday nights that they stuck it out through the rest of the week to get there. Those kids were at practice because they wanted to be, and that kind of desire is an individual thing.

But second, and maybe even more important, they were there because their coach was passionate about football. He made it seem like something worth doing, something great, something exciting. I was passionate about football. I didn't just like it—I loved it. The kids sensed that, and the kind of love and excitement I had about it made it exciting to them. They wanted to be a part of it.

As a typical football coach, I spent most of my time with the team. I'd put on shorts and do exercises with them. I'd run with them, work out on weights with them. On Friday night when they scored a touchdown, I'd jump up and down and celebrate with them. If we had a big loss, I cried with them.

You take the typical English teacher who sits down behind the desk, doesn't get involved with the kids, just bores you to death. I told my friend, "If you want to get kids excited about English, you get excited first. Maybe you need to jump up on top of the desk or throw an eraser or scream and yell. All of a sudden, you might see them get excited about English."

Don't ever be afraid to show emotion. You may lose by being too distant or too "professional," like the English teacher, but you won't ever lose by being too passionate. It's not a weakness, like some people think. It's one of your greatest strengths.

YOU MOTIVATE YOU

Nobody can motivate you but yourself. Some people tell me, "Art, you're a motivator. You get me ready to really *do* something." I believe all that will stay with you for a few days. But sooner or later, it all comes back to *you*. Last year I was speaking in Salt Lake City, and I found out that the week before there had been a bunch of motivational speakers at that same coliseum. They were charging around $200 for a two-day course. On impulse, I asked the people in our meeting if any of them had attended. Hands went up all over the place. Well, there's nothing wrong with getting motivated by a speech or having a motivational tape to play in your car. You can always use help. The problem is that many people think that getting pumped up for a few minutes will make them win. Listening to motivational speeches is enjoyable. But all that is only temporary. Something *inside* has to change.

I see so many men and women fail in this life waiting for somebody to motivate them. Nobody can motivate you. *You* have to motivate yourself. You've got to be excited about life, pumped up about life.

Fundamental #2: *Stop making excuses.*

An important part of having a positive attitude is refusing to look for or accept a reason *not* to do it. Many people think that just avoiding negatives is the answer, but actively pursuing positives has to be a part of your basic outlook on life.

UNWRITTEN LAW: *Life is 10 percent what you make it and 90 percent how you take it.*

I went to see two vice presidents in our company about six months after they moved to St. Louis. On the way back from the airport, one v.p. and his partner, who had moved from Colorado, began to tell me how tough it was in their new city. "Boy, Art, you see that license plate out there? In Missouri, the theme is 'show me.' These people are a little more skeptical than the people where I come from." One of them went on to explain that the people in Colorado believed a little quicker and bought a little quicker and came to work a little quicker. That was the reason business wasn't doing so well.

I listened for an hour or so, and then we picked up another couple. They were singing the same tune. They had moved from Jackson, Mississippi, and they were telling me the same thing. People in Mississippi were just a little quicker to make a decision, to buy, to come to work. The people in St. Louis were a little more difficult.

That afternoon we had a managers meeting, and I got up and told them about those conversations. I also told them that I'd been in Cleveland, Ohio, the day before, and the guy I stayed with there was telling me how much he loved Cleveland and how he was hoping to start doing well *soon,* but he had found that the folks in Cleveland were just a little different from the way they were in Atlanta. (Can you guess? They were a little more skeptical and a little less quick to buy!) I explained that the day before that I had been in Baton Rouge, and I heard the same thing there!

You know what? People are people everywhere. The guys who had moved to new areas were a little less confident, a little more hesitant, than they had been before in an area that was familiar to them. There wasn't any difference in the people in all those places. The difference was in their attitude.

Remember the unwritten law: *Life is 10 percent what you make it and 90 percent how you take it.*

Fundamental #3: *Always be "up."*

You can see life as a painful or a beautiful experience. You've got to make a decision to always be "up" about life— about your business, your family, your people.

Now, I know you're saying, "Art, it's easy for you to say that, but it's not so easy for me to do."

I didn't say it was easy. Experience has taught me that it's just human nature to worry. Every piece of flesh on this earth worries. That's just part of living.

You get scared and down and discouraged, and you think that means you're a failure. All that means is that you're a human being. You see, it's easier to be negative than positive. It's *tough* to stay excited. To be positive. To be happy. To continue to fight. Worrying is a part of human nature. You can beat human nature, but you must recognize that it won't happen overnight. You've got to work at it. The fact is, it's a waste of time, because *99 percent of the things you worry about never happen.* Don't waste your time!

UNWRITTEN LAW:	*Don't let the complainers, criticizers, and moaners change you and make you negative.*

Stanley Beyer, a great friend of mine and a huge success in his own right, made a tremendous speech to our company about maintaining a positive attitude. Stanley said, "People think that when you get to a successful position where you have money and recognition and success, everything is great and wonderful all the time. They think that we are positive all the time, that we don't have the same problems. But you know, all the great people I've ever known have these same problems. They are positive for only a certain period of time.

"At first, you're confident and positive for maybe a few seconds, and then maybe you get negative. Then you become a little more successful, and you become positive for a few minutes, then for a few hours, then for a few days. The most confident, successful, positive person I've ever known was that way for only a short period of time. Everybody has fears and doubts. Everybody goes into depressions. The most successful people in the world doubt whether they can make it or not. But the only way you can handle that is by having a positive attitude, knowing that if you just hang in there long enough, things will work out."

Ultimately, it doesn't matter what your problems are. Everybody has problems. The only thing that matters is how you look at your life, including your problems.

You can do two things to help yourself stay "up":

First, *don't let the losers, criticizers, and complainers change you and make you give up.* You've got to eliminate as many negatives from your life as possible. Some people just drain your batteries. They see the bad in everything. You know the type. You're in your office working, feeling fine, and they stop by to chat. They've got a dozen miserable stories to tell you about bad things that have happened. They tell you how everything at work is fouled up. They tell you about how difficult life is. After about ten minutes, you're ready to crawl in a hole and pull it in after you.

Don't listen to them. Make a point of staying away from those people. In a nice way, refuse to listen to all the bad news. You're probably saying, "Art, you're an insensitive low life." I'm not saying don't be sensitive to people who are really in trouble. I'm saying don't be taken in by people who complain as a way of life. Surround yourself with positive, excited, happy people who love what they're doing. Be an example of a positive attitude yourself.

Second, *pass negatives up and positives down.* This is something I constantly emphasize in our company. Whatever level you are in management, find someone at your level or above when you have a problem you need to talk over. Get it all out of your system. It works like a safety valve. That way, you're not tempted to pass your disappointments and frustrations down to the people you supervise. Someone at your own level or above is better able to cope with your negatives than someone junior to you who is looking to you for guidance and support. Your people should never see you negative. They should always see you "up."

Fundamental #4: *Make a total commitment.*

I talked earlier about the importance of commitment on your way to winning. Total commitment helps you maintain a positive attitude. It's amazing how you're able to turn problems into possibilities when you eliminate the option of giving up. If you're committed to win—no matter what—you'll have a totally different outlook on your life and your business. The *only* recourse to dealing with negatives is to turn them into positives.

UNWRITTEN LAW: *A total commitment gives you the extra ounce of courage that it takes to win.*

Paula Smith, one of our great national sales directors, was a college professor with two or three degrees in Georgia. After teaching for several years, Paula was burned out and frustrated. She was in her mid-thirties and had never married, but she had an adopted son. Paula decided she wanted out of education and into the business world. It would be more exciting, a change, and she could make more money than she could as a teacher.

Paula's uncle heard that she was going to leave teaching and told her to call me before she did anything else. When he explained that A. L. Williams sold term life insurance and investments, she said, "Well, teaching might be bad, but it isn't *that* bad! There's no way I'm going to sell insurance!"

In spite of her protests, Paula agreed to see me, just to please her uncle. To make a long story short, Paula decided to take a leave of absence from teaching and go to work with us.

The first eight or nine months were hard for her. At the end of ten months, she came to see me. In two months, her leave of absence would be up, and she had to go back to teaching or resign her position. She told me how much she loved the company and how badly she wanted to stay, but she just couldn't face losing her teaching job. What if something went wrong? What if she couldn't make enough money? How could she give up the security of that job for a job that paid commissions?

That was just the problem. As long as Paula knew she had something to go back to, she could avoid making a total commitment to A. L. Williams. She wasn't really giving it all she had. She had no intensity. She liked what she was doing, but she wasn't *excited* about what she was doing. Paula wasn't "turned on," intense and positive like you have to be to win.

I didn't hear from Paula for four or five weeks. Then one day, she called. She said, "Art, I haven't been able to sleep. I've had that security blanket in my mind, but you know what? I can't go back and teach. That's what I wanted to leave. I'm scared to death, but I'm going to do it. I don't know where and I don't know how or why, but I know that I'm supposed to be somebody."

Paula resigned her teaching job, picked up her son, and moved to Augusta, Georgia. Three months later, she was paid more in a single month than she had ever been paid before in a year. Three months after that, she did so well that she was promoted to regional vice president. Now, Paula's one of the top leaders in our company.

Total commitment. Until Paula burned her bridges and said, "Here is where I'm going to take my stand. Here is where I'm going to do something special," she did badly. But the minute she decided to go for it, her whole life changed. She couldn't afford to "play" at A. L. Williams any longer. She had to make it or break it, and there was no going back. When Paula made a total commitment to what she was doing, things started to fall into place.

Attitude Is Everything

I believe you can overcome every problem in life but an attitude problem. I've spent a lot of my adult life studying men and women and why most of them lose and only a few win. It took me a long time to really understand what a big part attitude played in success.

UNWRITTEN LAW: *Attitude isn't just a little thing; it's everything.*

I hope you're starting to realize that there's no trick to winning. It's an everyday, all-the-time thing. More than anything else, it's an attitude.

If you don't remember anything else in this book, remember the three rules that are critical to your success in all areas of life:

1. Always be positive.
2. Always be positive.
3. Always be positive.

CHAPTER NINE

Treat People "Good"

Treat others as you want them to treat you.
Luke 6:31

N o matter what your business or career is, you can't do it alone. The more success you have, the more likely it is that you will have other people on your "success team." How you treat those people can make the difference in whether your business takes off or falls flat. You must treat them with honesty and integrity before you can expect them to treat you in the same way.

You can be great in all the areas we've talked about so far—have great desire, have a big dream, be a crusader, have a great attitude—and still fail if you don't understand human nature. But before you can develop the art of people management, you may have to make some changes in your outlook.

You Must Believe in the Goodness of People

Before you can be successful, you must believe in the goodness of people. Unfortunately, most people don't. Most people have been so hurt and so disappointed by other people that they just can't believe that human beings have the potential to be good. Instead, they say, "Everybody's out to cheat me; everybody's out to take advantage of me. I'd better do it to them before they do it to me." People are skeptical of everybody and everything. Those beliefs won't work, though, if you want to build a team that will help you build your business.

You know, other people are pretty much like you. That's important to remember. Sure, there are some bad people in the world. But most of the time, the people you hire and deal with at your work are just as scared of being cheated by you as you are scared of being cheated by them. They've been hurt, too, and as much as you'd like to think they can tell you're different, they are just as hesitant to trust as you are. The best way to turn that situation around is to start understanding people and treating them the way you'd want to be treated.

Ed "Mugsy" Maguire spent most of his adult life on a New Jersey police force. He was a detective who worked seventy-five hours a week to make $22,500 a year. But it wasn't just a run-of-the-mill police job. Ed's job was extremely dangerous. On a daily basis, he dealt with the New Jersey Mafia. He spent his time looking for criminals and locking them up. He was constantly lied to, which made him suspicious of everyone. In fact, Ed was in a situation so dangerous that treating people "good" could get his head blown off. He was a tough guy surrounded by hardened criminals.

Believe me, when Ed joined our company, it wasn't because of our "pushing up people" philosophy! In fact, he was bitter when he came to seminars and heard others talking about treating people right. He felt it was "fake" and just "a bunch of hype" that didn't matter. Sooner or later, people would find out the "truth" about the business world. As for Ed, he wasn't going to be "taken in." He told himself that this was strictly a business venture, and that's where he drew the line.

Ed did OK at first. Nothing spectacular, but he made a living. But then he began to notice something. He saw people quit their full-time jobs and come to work with him in the business. He saw people trusting him and believing in him. And for the first time in his adult life, other people needed him to believe in them, too. Ed began to look at people as his friends. He started to really care about them and their families. He became the most positive and excited person you've ever met. And his business exploded. Everyone wanted to work with "Mugsy" Maguire. A few months later, he was promoted to vice president; three years after his promotion, he is one of our most successful—and respected—leaders.

You could *never* convince me that treating people good doesn't work. It worked for Ed, and I know it will work for you. You've just got to remember that inside *every* person is a winner who deserves to be treated as the most special individual on earth.

Nobody Wants a "Boss"

The last twenty-five years in this country, management has gotten confused with intimidation. Instead of people feeling like their boss is the leader of their team, most people look on their boss with fear! The word *boss* is a big mistake as far as I'm concerned. How many people can relax and do good work around someone whose job it is to "boss" them?

Somewhere along the way, businesses got the idea that the way to lead was through fear and intimidation. Nothing could be more wrong! Oh, fear works, there's no doubt about that. You can make people work by threatening them with their jobs. But you can't make them care about you and your business, and you can't build a business long-term without other people who are loyal and committed to the same cause you're committed to.

Management by intimidation is easy. Most people go that route because that's their idea of what a boss is "supposed" to do. It's also easier to intimidate people into performing than it is to take the trouble to spend time with them and build lasting relationships based on mutual respect.

UNWRITTEN LAW:	*Nobody needs a "boss"; everybody needs a leader.*

Gary Hazen worked for eleven years for a major pet food manufacturer. For five years, his job was to assign sales territories to different salespeople, making sure that the company was maximizing profits from each territory. Regardless of how much the person was making in a particular territory, he could be removed and handed another territory at a moment's notice if that switch would be a positive one for the company.

Gary saw some ugly things. People with a long work record and seniority had their territories cut or removed. Reps who were "making too much" (around $70,000), according to management, had their territories expanded, making it twice as hard next year for them to make the same amount of money. In extreme cases, management asked Gary to change a sales rep's territory entirely. All the sales reps lived in fear of management, in other words, Gary and the other sales managers.

As one of the "ax men," Gary reached the point where it was difficult for him to sleep at night. He dreaded going into the office and having to make decisions that hurt people he considered his friends. He knew that from year to year, they were afraid of their "boss." Gary even lived in fear that he would "get the ax," too.

It took about two years for Gary to "deprogram" when he joined our company. Like an infant, he had to start slowly and learn that you can be a successful businessman and still treat people good. Today, Gary's whole business revolves around making the people who work with him feel "special" and loved. Gary has learned that the more he helps others be successful, the more success he and his family experience! Gary is a national sales director with A. L. Williams, and one of the highest paid leaders in our company.

Praise Is "the Secret"

Things turned around for Gary, but how do *you* change yourself? How do you start your business on the road to success through the treat-people-good philosophy?

The answer is this: praise.

Nothing encourages people to work harder and produce quality results like having their accomplishments noticed and praised.

I call praise "the secret" because for many years this kind of motivation was one of the best-kept secrets in business. It's often ignored in standard management practice, but successful leaders have always known its value.

In the last few years, more managers have recognized the principle that great leaders—and great parents—have known all along: people respond better to praise than to punishment. When it comes to motivation, adults are no different from kids. If you criticize your children every time they make a mistake— tell them they're no good, they're sorry, they're lazy—you'll build kids who are unhappy and frustrated and who feel bad about themselves. Every child wants love and praise. If you praise kids and make them feel special, they'll be happy, self-confident, and ready to conquer the world.

UNWRITTEN LAW: *Genuine praise is one of the strongest forms of motivation.*

This principle works exactly the same way with adults. You read all the time about studies showing that people want more out of a job than just money. They work for all kinds of reasons—to be their own boss, to make money for their families—but one of the main things they want from their job is praise.

I believe that part of treating people good is making them feel good about their work. The best way of doing that is by rewarding the positive things they do instead of dwelling on the errors they make.

If you want someone to succeed, you start by praising him when he begins to do things right. In our business, for example, if you want to encourage a new sales rep to make sales appointments, you treat him like a hero. You take him out to lunch, tell everyone in the group about it, just generally put him on a pedestal. You may have made hundreds of appointments yourself, but you've got to remember that, to the new guy, making one contact may be the hardest thing he's ever done. He deserves to be rewarded for his achievement.

Everybody wants praise for a job well done. If you start praising for successful behavior, the person will want to get the same kind of recognition again. He'll be anxious to repeat the actions that gave him such good feelings of accomplishment. Then—and this is the important part—you won't have to make him go out and make more appointments. He'll be eager to do it again.

You know, in our company we get so used to the way we do things that we sometimes forget how it can be in the "real world." The other day I was talking with one of our top leaders who used to be associated with a major youth ministry. He said, "Art, I was there for five years, and for three years I was in a very important position in the ministry. In all that time, I had no personal contact with the leader of the ministry—not even a letter or a phone call—except to shake his hand twice." Think of that—all his hard work repaid with two handshakes in a five-year period!

Praise is more than a positive influence. It can make a life-changing difference. If you still doubt the value of praise, listen to the story of one of our national sales directors in Illinois who is a living example of the power of praise in a person's life.

Jeff was born and raised in the Chicago area. Both of his parents were the children of immigrants who had come to this country, worked hard, and made good. Jeff, his parents, and his older brother and sister had a comfortable life in a Chicago suburb.

When Jeff was only six years old, his father developed serious emotional problems. He couldn't work and soon lost his job. Things started to fall apart, and the family lost everything they had worked for. Six months later, Jeff's father committed suicide. Almost immediately, Jeff's mother had a nervous breakdown. She died two years later, when Jeff was eight years old.

Although Jeff had relatives in the area, local regulations at the time prevented the relatives from taking the children. They were eventually split up, with Jeff and his sister going into one orphanage, his older brother to another. In the years that followed, he spent time in an orphanage and two foster homes.

Finally, tired of always feeling displaced, unwanted—an outsider—Jeff packed his knapsack and hit the streets of Chicago. He was only twelve years old.

Alone in the city, he slept in abandoned cars or alleyways, and he stole to survive. Then came an "improvement." On the street, he met some "hippies" who were also drug pushers. They took him in, bought him a ten-speed bike, and gave him a job delivering the illegal drugs they sold around town. Whenever the police picked him up and put him in a juvenile center, he ran away again. It was a tough life, and the only rules were the rules of survival.

Jeff drifted, staying with first one person, then another. When he heard that his hippie friends had moved south to Elkville, he drifted that way. But there had been a change. The men had become Christians, given up the streets, and straightened out their lives. They shared what the Lord had done for them. Jeff, who had given little thought to religion in those tough years, thought they were crazy.

They took him to church with them, and the minister he met there became the major influence in Jeff's life. He took an interest in the boy and became his legal guardian.

Looking back now, Jeff can hardly speak about the tremendous difference this man made in his life. Jeff became a Christian, finished high school, and began to get his life on track.

Jeff remembers many things about this man who became like a father to him, but the thing he remembers most is the minister's approach. "I had long hair that I wore in a ponytail down my back. He was very conservative, and I asked him if I had to cut my hair. I was surprised when he said no. He didn't criticize me at all! He was so patient with me. He loved me and kept praising me. Whenever I did something wrong, he never concentrated on the negatives; he just told me that I had messed up and to dust myself off and start over again.

"I was a fighter," Jeff told me. "But I had no self-confidence. I had been living like an animal for a couple of years. People who knew me would say to me, 'Jeff, you'll never amount to a hill of beans.' I felt like the whole world was against me, so I was against the whole world. And then this guy took me in and said, 'Jeff, I believe in you. I know you can make it. You're as good as any of the other kids at school.'

"This man told me constantly that I could be whatever I wanted to be and that I had to forget the past and make a future for myself. He believed in me before I ever believed in myself."

Today, Jeff is a leader in our company. One of the reasons is the heartfelt lesson about praising people to success that he learned from the man who helped him change his life.

Folks, it doesn't take an M.B.A. to know a little about human nature and to know how to make people feel good about themselves.

UNWRITTEN LAW: *People will turn out the way you expect them to turn out.*

Your expectations as a leader are not lost on your people. People have a way of rising to the level that you set for them. If you have faith in their ability to develop new talents and improve performance, pretty soon they'll believe they can do it, too.

When I was coaching at Kendrick High School, we had two defensive tackles. One weighed about 165, and the other was about 175. If you know anything about football, you know that those are pitiful weights for defensive tackles. Most of the quarterbacks weighed more than that!

But we had those two guys, and that was that. It looked a little grim, but I made a point of making them feel that they were the toughest, roughest, meanest defensive tackles in our conference. I didn't lie to them, but whenever they did something right, I let them know how great it was. Every week, I'd wonder if they could hold on, and every week, those guys would go out there and play like they weighed 220 pounds. One of my assistant coaches at the time was a great guy, but he didn't think there was any way I could motivate those guys that way. But all they needed was to hear they were tough, and they'd go out there and be tougher than anybody on the field. I can tell you one thing, a lot of teams we played against would have sworn those guys weighed at least 250!

Don't Hide Your Praise Under a Basket—Praise in Public!

When you want to praise people for something they've done right, it's great to tell them, but even greater if you tell them in front of other people. To the people you're praising, it's even more pleasant, and to the people listening, it's motivation to do what it takes to get praise for themselves.

Public recognition is a principle that I live by in my business. Every meeting and convention has time set aside for recognizing people who have turned in a great performance. And I've found it's important to do more than just talk. Give people some memento of your recognition, like a plaque or a trophy. It's not the cost or size of the award that counts. It's the recognition. People love being singled out as being special.

When I first founded our company, we were planning a banquet at Stone Mountain, outside Atlanta. I wanted to reward people who were doing well with plaques, but at $25 each, I could afford only a few. One day it came to me. I would give T-shirt awards, just like I had given to the high-school football players when I was coaching. I went to the T-shirt store and bought twenty-five shirts.

I was so excited when I got to the house to pick up Angela for the banquet. I had a great feeling about the shirts. When Angela saw them, she was worried. "Art, you can't give grown-ups T-shirt awards. After all their work, they will expect something more than a T-shirt! They'll think you don't appreciate them." Well, I was concerned because Angela is right 99 percent of the time, but I just had a feeling about those shirts. I went ahead with my plan. I presented those "awards," and the people loved them. The slogans were simple, and some were funny. But they had powerful messages—things like "I Ain't Average" and "I Am Somebody." Today, over ten years and a lot of success later, I give lots of different awards. But the T-shirt awards are still the most popular . . . and the most fun.

People love recognition, and it doesn't matter if it's a $5 T-shirt. I can go to a meeting where people are making $500,000 to $1 million a year and give out T-shirt awards. Now, these people are the tops in the company, they have nice homes, and they've traveled all over the world. These adults, these leaders, come to meetings, and if they don't get an award, they get downright upset. It's amazing how much a T-shirt can mean to them and how determined they'll be to never miss getting another one.

That just shows that you can never get too much recognition. You can't get too "big" or too important for it or make so much money that you don't want to be appreciated and praised.

Recognition doesn't have to be an elaborate thing, either. It can be as simple as a handwritten note to say, "You're doing great. I'm proud of you," or a phone call to say, "Congratulations. I'm glad you're on my team."

UNWRITTEN LAW: *A great leader always gives his people credit for his success.*

A great leader understands that it's much more important for his people to receive recognition than for him to receive it. When I got my first head football coach's job, my high-school coach, West Thomas, called me and said, "Art, don't you ever forget this. A great head coach always gives his assistant coaches and players credit when the team wins. Don't ever miss an opportunity when you're talking to the press to give them recognition for the victory. But also remember that the head coach always takes all the blame when you lose."

That's good advice to apply to your business, too. When your company or your department does something special, give all the praise and all the credit to your people. You'll get your share of recognition for any job done well because you're the leader. But your people may be overlooked unless you point out their contributions. That lets them know that you're working for their success as well as your own. A great leader will never let his people think they are working just to help him get a promotion or make big money.

Praise Must Be Spontaneous

The real key to praise is that it's got to be spontaneous. You can't just say, "Well, I'm going to praise them once a week." You must really look for a genuine reason to praise them. Don't worry about overdoing it. You can't praise your employees too much. Have a good word for people every time you see them, and let them know whenever you notice something they've done well.

In a sense, you've got to become a goodwill ambassador. Always be the person who's saying something good about somebody. I know that it can be a challenge. Sometimes you have to look pretty hard to find something to praise. But it's there, somewhere, because everybody has good qualities.

Praise has to be natural. It has to be sincere and come from the heart. If you really love people, and care about them, you won't build a phony kind of relationship.

You Can't Change People's Basic Qualities

A primary mistake managers make is trying to change people. They focus all their energy on a person's weakest area and try desperately to turn that weakness into a strength. I am here to tell you that you can't do it. Everybody has strengths *and* weaknesses.

I was struck the other day by an extreme example of this. On one of the morning news shows was a young woman who had been born with no hands, but a tremendous spirit. She simply trained her body so she could survive without hands. With the aid of special equipment and a lot of determination, she could do everything the rest of us do—drive a car, cook dinner, hold down a job. She made the point many times that although she didn't feel the least deprived and had never seen herself as "handicapped" at all, other people persisted in seeing only her lack of hands. The young woman was leading a normal life and felt she had many strengths. *Other people* continued to dwell on her perceived "weaknesses."

Are you guilty of focusing all your energy on how you *would like* people to be instead of accepting them the way they are? Have you been dwelling on the "handicaps" and ignoring the progress? Everybody has at least one area in which he or she is really special. Find that area of strength, focus on it, build on it—and forget the weaknesses.

You can look for negatives, or you can look for positives. Looking for negatives builds an attitude of criticism and disapproval. Until you develop the ability to look for positives, you can't build a productive relationship.

You can't just pick out positives occasionally. You must do it consistently, every day, all the time, until it becomes a way of life. It can't be a part-time commitment.

The Other Side of Praise

When I talk about never criticizing, people always say, "But, Art, if you don't criticize, how do you show people that they're doing something wrong? Sometimes you have to do *something*."

True. Sometimes people do act in ways that aren't good for the team or the business. You have to let them know that you don't approve of their actions. Or you have to let them know that their performance isn't what it should be.

But you can do it without criticizing. This is what I mean by "the other side of praise." Just as people will do almost anything to get your praise, believe me, they will notice if they don't get it.

If someone on your team starts going downhill or doing badly at work, instead of criticizing that person, just praise somebody else. Praise is like love; you can't get too much, and when someone withdraws it, it just about kills you.

UNWRITTEN LAW: *Withdrawing praise is ten times more effective than criticizing.*

People hunger for praise so much, they'll do whatever it takes to get your praise and recognition again. And you haven't been forced to say anything mean or make any threats that cause bad relationships.

One Final Word About Criticism—Don't

Yes, you read it right. Don't criticize people when they aren't doing well. Let me put it more strongly. You'll never build a team—and you'll never win—by criticizing people. You can tell them ninety-nine positive things and one negative thing, and all they'll remember is the negative.

The best way to get people to see your point of view and to improve their behavior is to "hint and motivate." When someone has a problem, sit down and talk together. Talk about your own mistakes and let the person see that you have done some things wrong, too. Maybe you had problems in a similar area. Hint around about other times you've seen people doing things correctly.

Then, at the end of the meeting, motivate the individual. Acknowledge the efforts you've seen; express faith in the person's abilities. Leave the person with a good feeling.

How to Become a Master Motivator

1. Praise people for everything. Praise their attitude, their ideas, and their success. Nothing good is too small or too minor to praise!

2. Know the individual's first name, and use it! During my speeches, I use the first names of people I see in the audience. Talk about motivation!

3. Make sure everyone hears your praise. Sometimes the people who aren't being praised get as much motivation from it

as your hero. They'll give that extra effort so they'll be praised next!

4. Have fun with praise. Be creative with your recognition. I give six-foot trophies and door-sized plaques.

5. Use praise as a gentle nudge. I sometimes give awards like "I Almost Made It" or "Flash in the Pan." WARNING: *Never* give this kind of award unless the person has fantastic ability and will use the award as a challenge.

6. Use praise, *not* criticism, to get results. Don't fuss at the people who are doing it wrong. Praise the folks who are doing it right, and the other people will get the idea. For example, if sales are down, make heroes out of the top salespeople. This gets the nonproducers out there trying to earn praise.

7. Praise people when they are down and hurting. Know when your people are down, and be there to remind them of their dream and tell them they're special.

8. Praise must be sincere. You can never give too much praise as long as it is sincere and from the heart. Everybody has some good quality to praise. It may take you a while, but find it and praise it! WARNING: People can smell a phony a mile away.

9. Praise at home. These principles work wonders with your family life, too. Start with your spouse and children. Make them feel special.

10. Don't stop praising. You may have to praise people 1,000 times before they win, but if you only praise them 999, *you* lose.

Don't Be Afraid to Build Personal Relationships

Another fallacy taught in some business school courses is that managers must keep their distance from their employees. Nonsense! Your people are the lifeblood of your company. Their lives and careers are directly related to your business success.

Today, at our company, everybody—from the receptionist to the officers—calls me "Art." I wouldn't dream of expecting anyone I work with every day to call me "Mr. Williams." I want the people in A. L. Williams to feel like they can walk up to me and say "Hello" without being afraid.

Folks, icicles don't have many friends, and they don't get much loyalty. People ask me all the time, "Art, how do you build personal relationships?" Well, the idea that people have to ask says a lot about what's happened to us since we took the "heart" out of business.

Following these simple guidelines will mean more to your business than learning how to be tough.

Guideline #1: *Others don't care how much you know until they know how much you care.*

You may be a business genius, but if your people don't know you care about them, your business won't get far. Know your people by name; know their families; get to know them as people and really care about them. That doesn't mean you have to be a pushover, though. You can be tough and still care.

I'll never forget Coach Tommy Taylor. He was like a second daddy to me. Coach Taylor was tough. Christmas holidays were always basketball tournament time, and even during the holidays, we'd have to practice twice a day. On game days, we even had a practice, which was unheard of at that time. Sure, we griped about having to practice over the holidays. But we never had any bad feelings toward Coach Taylor, even though he was tough. You know why? Because we all knew that he cared about each and every one of us. We always knew that he'd do anything he could for us and that he wanted more than anything for our high-school athletic experience to be wonderful. He really loved coaching, he loved *us,* and we knew it.

SPECIAL NOTE: You've got to be sincere. You can't "fake it." You have to develop a genuine caring interest in people.

Guideline #2: *Live with your people through good times and bad times.*

Don't just support your people when everything's going

great. The deepest relationships are formed in the tough times. If you stick with people then, you'll build a relationship that will stand up against any business problem. Remember what Dr. Robert Schuller says: "Tough times don't last, but tough people do."

Guideline #3: *Don't be afraid to show emotion.*

Most people today are so afraid to show emotion in their business lives that they end up acting like they don't have any at all. Be human. Don't be afraid to laugh or cry. Touch people; hug them. I haven't met a single person yet who doesn't like being hugged.

Ginny Carter was one of the original eighty-five people who came with me to form A. L. Williams. She and I have been through a lot. Recently, she was asked about working with me, and she told about how I used to stop by the Dairy Queen in the early days and get giant hot fudge sundaes for all of us to eat when we were having a meeting. Such a little thing, but somebody remembered it ten years later. Does that tell you something about how much your caring and concern—in the tiniest ways—can mean to people? Just as people never forget harsh words, they never forget a kindness. Think about it.

Guideline #4: *Make an "unconditional" commitment.*

The people who work with you in your business need the same kind of commitment that you make in other areas of your life. All parents know that sometimes the kids need you and sometimes they want to "do it themselves." Sometimes they're wonderful, and sometimes they're a pain. It's the same with your people.

The difference is that many leaders like their people in the good times, but drop them whenever they get a little difficult. You wouldn't do that with your kids, would you? The people you choose for your team deserve the same "unconditional" commitment that you give other important people in your life.

I love my wife more than anyone on earth, but I don't "like" her every day. She feels the same way about me. I drive her crazy with things like playing country music. She gets on my nerves by forgetting things like leaving the cap off the toothpaste. But these little things are something we accept because in the overall picture, they're not important. Angela and I have made a total commitment to our marriage. Winning in business demands a total commitment just like winning in a marriage demands total commitment.

UNWRITTEN LAW: *A position doesn't make a person; a person makes a position.*

People make positions special; it's not the other way around. Nothing is free to a leader. You can't demand respect, loyalty, trust, or love from your people. You must earn it.

You can't fake honesty, integrity, or belief. You must be sincere.

As a leader, you've got to remember that it's not good enough just to be right. Your people must *believe* you're right before you can gain their trust and respect.

Remember the People Quotient

When it's all said and done, products and services don't win for you. Business plans don't win for you. People win. Your people are your most valuable asset. They'll help you take your business to the heights. They deserve your best because you're asking them to do *their* best for you.

Stop worrying about the old model of bosses. Forget the fear factor and add the human factor to your business. Treat people "good," and they'll respond to you and your business with a new kind of commitment and enthusiasm. You'll feel better about your business and about yourself.

CHAPTER TEN

Never Give Up

When nothing seems to help, I go and look at a stonecutter, hammering away at his rock, perhaps a hundred times without as much as a crack showing in it.
Yet at the hundred and first blow it will split in two, and I know it was not that blow that did it—but all that had gone before.

Jacob Riis

Quitting is easy. Anybody can quit. In fact, most people do. If everybody out there was tough, dedicated, and determined, the winner's circle would be a lot more crowded than it is. But it isn't crowded because most people won't stick it out long enough to win. If you have the courage and strength to hang on and refuse to give up, you dramatically increase your chances of winning.

There are some good reasons not to quit. The first reason is that losing, like winning, is a habit. All quitters are good losers. If you quit and give up in one instance, it's easier to do the second time, and even easier the third. Pretty soon, quitting is a way of life.

The second, and most important, reason is that you wanted to be somebody, to do something special with your life. You didn't want to be like most people. You didn't want to be average and ordinary. If you quit, your opportunity to achieve your dreams is lost. Chances are, if you quit once, you'll never bounce back. You'll have to live with being average and ordinary for the rest of your life. What's worse, you'll have to live with that feeling of failure.

Nothing makes the tough times easier. But there are some "do's" and "don'ts" that can help you keep your eye on the ball and keep you hanging on when you feel that every hope is lost. Believe it or not, I want to show you that even though you may sometimes think it's hopeless, there are some good reasons for *not* quitting.

One of the first people I hired when I started my business was Bobby Buisson. He was a coach, too, and I knew he was a good, quality person. Bobby was young with a wife and two kids, and he was barely surviving on his coaching salary.

Bobby gave up his coaching job to come full-time with our new company. There was one major problem. Outside the coaching area, Bobby was so shy he couldn't talk to anybody. It was difficult for him to make a sales presentation. He'd hang around the office all day instead of going out on sales calls. When he did finally succeed in setting up appointments, he'd start getting nervous hours before he was supposed to go. By the time the appointment came around, he was in a cold sweat.

He was really suffering. He was miserable at what he was doing, even though he believed in our crusade with all his heart. It actually hurt me to see him try to make a living.

The first four months, he made very few sales. I knew he was hurting, and hurting bad. We had all started to wonder why he continued to put himself through the torture.

But you know what? No matter how bad it was, he believed he had finally found an opportunity, a chance for a coach to do something special with his life.

Although he was dying inside every time he called someone on the phone or went to a house to give a presentation, he just kept going back, over and over and over. Since he wasn't very convincing, he wasn't getting many "yeses." His world consisted of nothing but "noes." His days were spent in sheer terror at the office, trying to get appointments, and his nights were filled with rejection. Every day he was paying a killing price. It was brutal.

Still, every day Bobby got up and came into the office. Every day he forced (and I do mean forced) himself to call people on the phone; every night he forced himself to go on presentation calls.

Bobby had a crusade and a dream of financial independence for his family. He had a determination and will to win like I've never seen. The guy just wouldn't give up, no matter what.

Finally, after many months, he started getting some decent appointments. Occasionally, he'd manage to make a few sales. Then a few more. Once he got the hang of it, he was unstoppable. When he finally started making a little money, he was the happiest guy in the world.

I don't think there was any price Bobby Buisson wouldn't have paid for success. The first year, he made less money than he had earned as a coach. The second year, he equaled his coaching income. How many people would have paid that price? But he stuck it out, and two years later, his determination was earning him several times his coaching salary.

Today, Bobby Buisson is a national sales director, one of our company's highest management positions, and a multi-millionaire. Bobby often travels with me to company conventions where he's a favorite speaker because he can relate so well to the person out there who's just getting started and having a tough time.

Bobby suffered personal humiliation and rejection; he suffered the pain of knowing that his family was struggling while he went in search of a better life. But Bobby was unwilling to quit. He kept on going through the pain and the difficulties.

The Truth about Failure

So many people have such a fear of failure that they never do anything. That keeps them from experiencing failure, but it sure does limit their success, too. If you have a goal of doing great things, you're bound to have failures somewhere along that path.

I've been in this business a long time, and I still mess up every week. It used to be every day, but I got better! Everybody loses every now and then. Look at the Super Bowl. Those are the two best teams in the nation. But one of them has to lose. No matter what your level in business, sometimes you're going to have a setback.

The important thing to remember is that *failure is only the end if you let it be*. If one failure causes you to give up, you have really lost. Bob Miller, a great friend of mine in the business, has a saying that I love. I guess I'd call it an unwritten law.

UNWRITTEN LAW: *Failure is the halfway mark on the road to success.*

It's a good thought. Failure is just one stage you'll go through on your way to the top. Everybody who's ever been a winner has experienced it at one time or another. In his book *The Renewal Factor*, Robert Waterman refers to failure as a "mind-set" rather than an absolute, and he refers to a study showing that great leaders never used the word *failure*. Instead, they used words like *mistake* and *glitch*. They simply never viewed themselves as having *failed*. We could all take a lesson from that. Failure is never the end of the road—unless we give up.

Refusal to Fail

Frances Averett joined our company a few years ago. Her husband had owned a plant nursery and done fairly well. When his health began to fail, however, the nursery business went downhill. Everything the Averetts had was tied up in the business.

The Averetts had five children, and Frances had stayed home to care for them. When her husband became ill, she was forced to jump in and try to save the business. She couldn't.

When she came into our business, Frances became the breadwinner. She had no business experience, five children to raise, and over $400,000 of debt hanging over her head. Nobody could have been more down or suffering the bad effects of a failure than this family.

But Frances was determined not to declare bankruptcy; she didn't want that blemish on their name. She was scared to death; nobody would have faulted her if she had just given up. But she was determined not to make failure the final chapter in her family's life.

Frances fought all the way, and the adversity she suffered only seemed to make her stronger, more determined.

In December 1988, Frances expects to make the final payment on the original debt. Today, she is a superstar in our company and has built a business for herself that will prosper for years to come.

Just a few years ago, anyone would have said that Frances and Lee, her husband, had failed. Nobody would say that today as the Averetts enjoy a financial freedom they never dreamed possible.

Failure doesn't have to be final if you don't give up. Trying is so much better than never failing.

Keep On Keeping On

When things are tough, we tend to get discouraged and do less than we've done before.

Wrong!

That is the worst time to slow down. The best cure for discouragement is to double and triple your efforts. Your goal should be to experience some success—even if it's small—to calm your fears and motivate you to keep going.

Even if you're frustrated and don't know exactly what you should be doing, do *something*. Nothing could be worse than standing still and watching your dreams collapse around you. Every time you generate activity—of any kind—you're adding another building block to the structure of your business. Keep pushing.

Going for It One More Time

Five years ago, Frank and Nyla Caler were destitute. Frank had owned a business previously, and he had enjoyed some success. But when the economy shifted, Frank's business started failing. They didn't take bankrupcy but chose to pay out the debt when the business failed. At the time, Frank was in his late forties.

When he came to A. L. Williams, he and Nyla had just moved to Colorado Springs to start a new life. Because he was new to the area, he had no credibility in the community and no contacts. He and Nyla had no cash and no credit. And they had a million "gotchas" hanging over them. It looked like they were just too far down to recover.

Frank saw our company as his last chance. For four years, he struggled. It was touch and go. Eventually, Frank was able to overcome his bad financial situation. Gradually, his business started to take off. His fifth year, he started to show signs of being a real winner.

The secret to Frank and Nyla's success was that they didn't give up when their world was falling apart. They plunged right in and started over. The return wasn't instant, and most people would have thrown in the towel. After all, how much should anyone have to take? Instead, they stuck it out. Frank knew it might be his last opportunity, and nothing was going to make him quit. Today, Frank is a vice president with the company, with a healthy income and a booming business.

Hanging on in the tough times—that's the part of success stories you usually don't hear about. But success is almost never "instant," although movies and TV tend to make us think that. Almost every story of true success also contains a story of great trial and sacrifice.

What to Do When You Want to Quit

You've worked hard. You know you've got the desire. You have a dream to inspire you and a crusade for a cause that's bigger than your business. Still, nothing seems to be working.

You've run head-on into the situation that you've had nightmares about. This is the time that shows what you're really made of. You're facing the toughest challenge you'll ever have in your business life. And you're facing the biggest temptation you'll ever have—the temptation to quit.

This is also the time that separates the winners from the losers.

I know about this period firsthand. When I was first trying to get my business going, there were a bunch of nights that I laid my head on the pillow feeling that the game was over. I couldn't see how I could pull it out one more time. I couldn't find any possible solution to my problems.

Thank God, I didn't quit during one of those times that I wanted to so bad I could taste it. But I know how it feels. At times that temptation can be almost overwhelming.

Whenever you bump up against one of those tough times, use these three fundamentals to help you "hang tough."

Fundamental #1: *Use the magic of thirty days.*

One of the best ways to keep on keeping on when you're experiencing tough times is to set specific short-term goals. We've already seen the advantages of setting long-term goals (my $300,000 goal for financial independence). Short-term goals are just as important.

We talked earlier about setting up little successes for yourself so your long-term goals don't seem so overwhelming. When things are going badly, these little victories can mean the difference between giving up and seeing enough hope to help you hang on until things get better.

When you feel like quitting, make one last surge with a thirty-day goal. It has to be a fairly tough goal; the purpose here is to revitalize your business or your life. It's not the time for a mediocre effort. Set a stiff goal and plan to do it for thirty days straight. I don't know what the magic of thirty days is, but I've learned from experience that, for some reason, that length of time works best. It's short enough for you to see an end in sight, and it's long enough to allow you to build some momentum.

UNWRITTEN LAW: *Almost anyone can do almost anything for thirty days.*

I know that a blitz is the last thing you feel like doing when times are tough. But you can do anything if you know it's for a short period of time. If your business needs a shot of adrenaline, it's the best thing you can do.

In the sales area, I'll counsel a guy who's been making four or five sales a month to set a goal of ten sales. That's a stretch; I know it will take a lot of work. But if the person can reach that goal for one thirty-day period, it's sure to set his business on a stronger course. Often, it gives him the little extra edge he needs to get things going again.

Go for it. I've seen it work thousands of times. It's the best way I know to stop thinking about quitting and *do* something that will create enough success to eliminate the thought altogether.

Fundamental #2: *Devise a system of reward and punishment.*

Reward and punishment go hand in hand with goal setting. When you set goals, you're making a commitment. You've got to have a system that will force you to stick to that commitment. (It's human nature to get tired and let our goals slide. A system of reward and punishment is a way to beat the natural tendencies of human nature.)

I first used the reward-and-punishment method when I coached football. At our victory meeting on Thursday, before the game on Friday night, I'd tell my guys, "Let me remind you of our goals. If you go out there tomorrow night and give it everything you've got and play as good as you can play and we beat the other team by more than 21 points or we have a great defensive game and hold the other team scoreless, we'll go out in shorts Monday for a light workout. Just think, Monday afternoon when the sixth period bell rings, and you're walking down to the gym holding hands with that little girlfriend, you'll see Coach Williams standing there with a smile on his face. We'll go out and loosen up for thirty or forty minutes. Man, that's living.

"But let's say you go out there tomorrow night and slop around. You just show up and we win by less than 21 points, or we win but let the other team score. Monday when the sixth period bell rings and you're walking down the hall with that little girl, you'll see Coach Williams at the dressing room door with a frown on his face. Instead of putting on shorts, you'll put on that old, heavy, stinkin' uniform, and we'll practice for two or three hours. Instead of ten wind sprints, we'll run forty-two.

"But picture this. Let's say you go out there tomorrow night, and you really slop it up and you lose. Then I'll see you at practice bright and early Saturday morning!"

Man, everybody hated those Saturday sessions, but it sure was an added incentive to get out there and give it everything they had on Friday night!

The concept of reward and punishment is one of those "head" techniques that helps you to get going and keep going when you don't really want to. If you set goals and nothing happens when you don't meet them, what's the use of having them at all?

You may think it sounds "Mickey Mouse," but it works!

Boxing great Muhammad Ali admitted to hating the grueling preparation for a fight. "I hated every minute of the training," Ali once said. "But I said, 'Don't quit. Suffer now and live the rest of your life as a champion.'"

Fundamental #3: *Give your efforts time to compound.*

The biggest frustration I have when I see people quit is that, oftentimes, they were so close to a turnaround it was unbelievable. They couldn't see it, but if they had just hung on a little bit longer, their business would have started to fall into place. More often than not, the problem is impatience. It's not that they've failed totally; it's that they haven't succeeded fast enough.

I'm sure you're familiar with the "magic of compound interest." This is the simplest concept in the world, but very few people undersand it. It's the most unbelievable law in the financial world. The magic of compound interest is what happens when you put time to work for you.

$1,000 LUMP-SUM INVESTMENT
(Invested One Time Only)

INTEREST	NUMBER OF YEARS					
	20	30	40	50	60	70
5%	$2,653	$ 4,321	$ 7,039	$ 11,467	$ 18,679	$ 30,426
10%	6,727	17,449	45,259	117,390	304,481	789,747

You'd think that to get the difference between 5 percent and 10 percent you'd just multiply by two. Wrong! The difference is staggering. That's why I call it "magic"!

"Compounding" works in effort, too. I said earlier that more than 90 percent of all businesses fail because most people get out of business and quit before they give their efforts time to compound. The first year that A. L. Williams was in business, we promoted only one vice president in our field force; ten years later, we promoted over one hundred per month. The first few years, our sales numbered in the hundreds; ten years later, we have over a million policyholders. In those early days, none of our people were even close to six-figure incomes; today, we have new additions each month to our $100,000 club. It was discouraging, sometimes, in those early years. But we kept pushing, increasing our efforts, and we hung on until those efforts had time to compound.

Give yourself *time* to succeed. Every contact you make, every client you see, every personal relationship you build, is part of the "investment" you make in your business. Over a period of time, these investments pay off. One client refers you to another. Someone you meet at a business luncheon remembers you and calls you when he needs your service; a phone call to one person generates business from that person's next-door neighbor. Each and every act you perform as a part of your business is a building block for the future.

(Remember our unwritten law: it takes three to five years to become established in business.)

Reasons Not to Quit

You may not notice it in the tough times, but chances are you've already come a long way from where you were when you started out on this new course.

✔   You've learned a lot; your experience has developed you into someone with a better chance of success than you had before. If you quit now, you've made that progress for nothing.

✔   You've paid a price. Think of all the sacrifices you've made trying to "go for it." If you quit now, all that you've worked so hard for and suffered for will mean nothing.

✔   You've set goals and made plans that involved your whole family. Can you live with yourself if you fold up your tent and go home?

Maybe you haven't given yourself enough time to let the principle of compounding take place.

The Tough Truth about Success

Now it's time to get down to the nitty-gritty. I never said that making it was going to be easy. I just said it was going to be worth it. I want you to read this book and see yourself as one of those people who want to "be somebody" more than anything. I want to motivate you to go for it. But I don't want to tell you it's all roses. It's not.

This is a tough chapter, and I want to talk tough. The following points aren't the most positive points in this book, but I know from experience that they're true. That doesn't mean you can't survive; I just want you to know the facts so you'll realize that your situation is no worse than everybody else's. And I want to try to prevent you from giving up when you encounter these realities.

Let's tell it like it really is.

Fact #1: *You never get used to rejection.*

When I found out about term insurance and made that my personal crusade, I thought that because I could see the "rightness" of the cause, everybody else would see it immediately, too.

Wrong! It didn't happen. A lot of people thought I was nuts. People just didn't want to be bothered. I was so sure I was right that I wasn't prepared for the powerful impact of people looking me in the eye and telling me they didn't want what I was selling. I wasn't prepared for the look on people's faces that said, "I don't believe you. I'm not interested."

UNWRITTEN LAW: *Just because you love what you're doing doesn't mean that everybody's going to love it, too.*

Everybody is not just like you. Some people are smarter, and a whole bunch of people are dumber. But even though you know you're right, don't expect the world to automatically jump on your bandwagon. That doesn't mean you shouldn't keep pushing, keep doing what you know is right for you.

When you face rejection, just remember all the people who do believe in you and listen to that little voice inside that says, "I know I'm right, and nothing will keep me from succeeding."

Fact #2: *Things are never as good as they seem or as bad as they seem.*

When things are going good, you can never assume that means you're home free. When things are going bad, you can't assume that your business is shot and your career is over. This business of life is nothing but a business of momentum.

You might be one day away from losing a top salesperson or suffering a financial setback or another disaster that could put you in a tailspin. So when things are going good, get all you can get.

By the same token, when things go down, don't let it kill you. You could be one appointment away from being on a high again. This business of winning calls for you to be an eternal optimist. The next day might set you off on a new path to greater success. Don't give up. You just have to keep on trucking.

During the good times, don't get complacent. During the bad times, don't start doubting whether you are going to do it or not. Stay inspired.

Fact #3: *Before you can be good, you've got to be bad.*

I guess we'd all like to think we've got what it takes to go after success and do *everything* right. Maybe there are a few people who are able to do almost anything. For most of us, though, we have to slug our way through the learning process.

Expecting to start out a winner is usually unrealistic. My first year in the sales business, I wanted to throw up every day. Every day I told myself I was going to go out and get a good job.

But instead I just hung on, and eventually, it got easier. I learned a lot, and I improved.

Remember, before you can be great, you've got to be good. Before you can be good, you've got to be bad. But before you can even be bad, you've got to *try*.

| **UNWRITTEN LAW:** | *Winners are* **made, not born.** |

If you're just trying right now, you're on your way. Don't worry about it if you know you aren't the greatest. You'll get there.

It's essential to have big dreams and big goals. But it's also important to remember that everything doesn't always go just the way you imagined it. So many people give up because the reality of their new adventure doesn't quite meet up with the beauty of their dream. That doesn't mean there was anything wrong with the dream. It just means that in real life we have to put up with a less-than-perfect world.

You can cope. There are some tricks that make it a little easier to keep a positive attitude and stay "up" most of the time.

Don't Compare Yourself to Others

A little competition is always healthy, but you can go too far. It usually works like this. You go out there and find something to dedicate your life to, and you're really on the road to greatness. You've made the commitment; you're doing the right kind of thing; you're making some money. You feel like you're really on your way.

Then one weekend, you run into an old friend, and he's doing three times better than you are. He's got a new car and a new house and more money than you ever dreamed of. All of a sudden your whole tune changes. You say, "Man, what a dud I am. Nobody has to pay the price I'm paying. Will I ever get there?" It literally kills you. Maybe you don't even have one client yet, and you see some other guy in your field who's complaining because he's got so many he can't take care of them all. You say, "Who's trying to punish me? I'll never get there." You begin to say, "That guy was just born great. He doesn't have to pay the price I'm paying." Wrong. Everybody pays the price. All those people paid their price somewhere along the way.

Give yourself a chance. I tell the people at my company that the millionaires of tomorrow are on the bottom of the leader's bulletins today. And I believe that. It's like the old saying, "You don't have to always have the lead if you have the heart to come from behind."

Wherever you are on your road to winning, even if you're just getting started, be proud of it. You don't have to apologize for anything.

I know from my athletic background that the greatest successes in later life were always the people who wanted to be great athletes but didn't have the ability. They tried so hard, and they learned all the values that gave them the chance to be winners later on. Sometimes the kids who have all the ability don't have to work that hard, and they don't learn the lessons that will help them down the road.

I heard about some advice a Yale University president gave to a former president of Ohio State. "Always be kind to your *A* and *B* students," he said. "Someday one of them will return to your campus as a good professor. And also be kind to your *C* students. Someday one of them will return and build you a $2 million science laboratory."

Don't Get Discouraged

My friend Bill Anderton tells a great story about this problem. It seems that one day the devil decided to go out of business, and he decided to sell all his tools to whomever would pay the price. On the night of the sale, they were all attractively displayed. Malice, hate, envy, jealousy, greed, sensuality, and deceit were among them. To the side lay a harmless wedge-shaped tool, which had been used much more than any of the rest.

Someone asked the devil, "What's that? It's priced so high."

The devil answered, "That's discouragement."

"But why is it priced so much higher than the rest?" the onlooker persisted.

"Because," replied the devil, "with that tool I can pry open and get inside a person's consciousness when I couldn't get near with any of the others. Once discouragement gets inside, I can let all the other tools do their work."

Discouragement is at the bottom of so many negative actions. You'll face it every single day of your life. How you handle discouragement each and every day goes a long way in determining your success or failure in reaching your dreams. Keep your dream alive, strive to reach your goals, have a positive winning attitude—and never, ever give up.

Don't Almost *Do Enough*

Most people *almost* work hard enough to win.
Most people *almost* hang in there long enough to win.
Most people *almost* have enough determination to win.

UNWRITTEN LAW: **Most people do almost enough to win.**

Wouldn't it be easier to stick out a tough situation and make it work than to go back and sit down in your easy chair in front of the TV and know that you had blown your last chance?

Chances are, if you give up, you'll never be able to forgive yourself for it. When you feel like giving up, make a promise to yourself to hang on one more week, one more month, and when that time's up, do it again.

In my "perfect" playbook that I was so proud of in my early days as a head football coach, there were no bad plays. I spent hours analyzing our game films and figuring out what plays worked best. Every play was designed to be a great play. Every single one was designed to put points on the board.

I used to tease my players and tell them that they were the luckiest team in the world. I told them that they had two tremendous advantages over the competition: they had a coach who was the best play caller in the business, and they had the best plays in football. I told them it was impossible for me to call a bad play, and we had no bad plays, so they could just get ready to put those points on the board.

I said, "Boys, these plays are guaranteed to score a touchdown every time . . . as long as you don't mess them up."

That was the catch.

If you've got a hundred plays in a football game, with two teams evenly matched, how many plays really end up as a touchdown? At the most, you might actually see two or three great passes or great runs. How many times do you see somebody miss a block or drop a pass or make a fumble? Only about 95 percent of the time, that's all.

But you know what?

The coach who wins the game just keeps calling the plays. He keeps calling them and calling them, even if 95 percent of them don't work. The players just keep thinking they're going to win.

In your business life, 95 percent of the things you do aren't going to work. You can't look inside a man or woman and tell who's going to buy. You can't make a presentation and guarantee that everybody's going to love it. You can't open a store and know that hundreds of customers are going to flock into it.

Don't get discouraged. Don't *almost* do enough. No matter how tough it gets, just keep calling the plays. Somebody's going to score sooner or later, and it might as well be you.

Keep calling 'em!

CHAPTER ELEVEN

The "Do It" Principle

Don't wait for your ship to come in; swim out to it.
Anonymous

You and I both know there's something inside you that won't let you be average and ordinary. That's why you're reading this book. Some of you will probably finish this book, then go to the bookstore and buy another one and read that. Most of you will put off trying to change your life for a few days and say to yourself, "I'll start next week." But some of you, a very select few, will put this book down and go "do it."

All the other principles in this book won't do you a bit of good if you never act on them. There's got to be action for you to win. Talk is cheap. Everybody talks a good game. But a winner goes out and does something.

As I mentioned earlier, a favorite speech I give around the country is my "do it" speech. People are always coming up to me and saying, "Art, what do you mean when you say to 'do it'?" Do *what*?"

I simply respond, "It."

"But, Art, what *is* it?"

"It's just *it*."

Sometimes, people get a little frustrated. They want me to tell them exactly how to "do it." But I can't do that because every single situation is different, and I don't know what *you* will have to do to make it.

The "it" in "do it" isn't any *one* thing. When you "do it," you just go out there and do whatever it takes for you to win. When it comes right down to it, a book can make it easier, but a book can't "do it" for you. Your spouse can't and your friends can't. You—and only you—can go out there and make your dream a reality.

Larry Weidel, one of my great friends in Greensboro, North Carolina, figured out what I meant by "do it" several years ago. Larry had been an engineer in the construction business back in 1973 and 1974 in Atlanta. His business went under when the real estate market hit rock bottom.

So Larry began to sell insurance and investments, and he really struggled. He had never sold anything in his life. His first four years in the business he could just barely make it. He did just enough to keep food on the table. But he was such a good, loyal, committed, honest guy that when A. L. Williams was getting ready to open the state of North Carolina, we asked Larry if he'd like to go.

His first six months there were a total disaster. Everything he touched fell apart; he just couldn't get it going. We had a convention at a beach resort in Georgia, and Larry had to borrow $100 from his manager to be able to attend. All the couples were having a great time, but Larry was so broke he couldn't even bring his spouse.

About three or four months later, things started to change for Larry. He got a promotion and started to make a lot of money. I couldn't have been more pleased than if my own son, "little Art," had made it.

One of the greatest honors in our company is to have a chance to speak at conventions. Because Larry was doing so well, I asked him to speak at our next one. I told him to take an hour—he took two. He began by handing out all this stuff for people to look over as he spoke. Then he proceeded to give a big speech about the "system" he had developed and about how this system had been the key to his success. He claimed that he had gone back and committed to a system, and after using that system for thirty days, he started winning. He said that he won because of the system.

When Larry's speech was finally over, everyone applauded and seemed to be nodding in agreement over Larry's great "system." I stepped up to the podium and said, "Wait a minute. Larry, you're dead wrong."

And I told Larry what I tell others who think they've come up with some master plan on how to get clients or how to find good recruits. You see, folks, a system isn't the key.

You know why Larry won? Because he had been struggling for four years and he went to the convention and he was broke and he saw everybody else getting awards. He was with happy, turned-on people who were making money and having success, and he was about as low as he could get. All of a sudden, he made up his mind for the last time that he was going to quit running. He was going to quit starving. He decided that he was put here to win. And he went back and began to "do it."

Larry developed a system, but the reason for his newfound success wasn't the system. Larry Weidel was sick and tired of being average and ordinary. So Larry learned to "do it," to do whatever it took to win.

Competition Is the Best Thing that Can Happen to You

There's one thing I wish for you that will help you "do it." I don't know what your business is, but I hope that whatever it is, you've got a competitor. Now I'm not talking about comparing yourself personally with others. I'm talking about healthy business competition with a competitor. Without competition, it's a thousand times tougher to motivate yourself. But if you've got someone to compete against, you've got an automatic motivator.

Not everyone feels like I do. You see, some people like to use competition as an excuse for *not* "doing it." They like to tell themselves, "Well, I just can't compete with those guys. There's no point in trying."

I was speaking at one of our seminars in Dallas, Texas, and a regional vice president came up to me on stage the first night and handed me a packet of stuff from one of our competitors. He said, "Boy, Art, you ought to see what they say about A. L. Williams. Boy, they are sure running us down."

Well, that was the wrong thing to say to someone like me. I looked at him, and I said, "What do you mean? Did you think it was going to be easy? Did you think our competition was going to roll over and play dead? They're not going to say, 'Welcome A. L. Williams! Thank you so much! Hallelujah! Take our business! You're wonderful for knocking us down, for making us compete, for telling consumers there's another way.'

"Did you think Prudential would use all their advertising money to show a little Prudential rock with a white surrender flag floating down the river?"

Of course not! We may be convinced that what we're doing is right, but that doesn't mean that the competition isn't ever going to get any customers.

I'll tell you what, though. Our competition is the best thing that's ever happened to us. I thank the Lord every day for other insurance companies. I live to be able to get up every day and say that our company is number one, that we beat the big insurance companies. When I don't feel like "doing it" some mornings, all I have to think about to get me going is the competition.

So what if it's tough? So what if your competition wants to knock you down? That's what I love about the free enterprise system. I want all of us to have a chance to go as far as we are capable of going on our own merit.

That's what is so great about your opportunity in America. Your success doesn't depend on anybody else but you—how much you love it, how much you want it, how much you believe in it, how determined you are to win.

Yet you can't reach your goals unless you're willing to get out of bed every morning and go out there and compete. You know why that gives you a head start on winning?

Most people aren't willing to compete. I said this earlier in the book. You beat 90 percent of the people by working hard, finding something you believe in, and being a person of honesty and integrity. Most people aren't willing to do the tough kinds of things it takes to win. About 99 percent of all the businesses in America today are crying and dying and making excuses and are frustrated like never before.

The people who are real winners aren't looking for handouts; they're looking for opportunities. If you give them an opportunity to do something special with their lives, they'll jump all over it. You know why you're different if you're reading this book, if you're taking the time to read it and think about it? Because most people in America aren't willing to go out there again and take a chance and lay it on the line and believe in something.

I'm not the only one who feels this way. Look around you. People who are successful in business love the thrill of competition, and they've gotten tougher and tougher in their battle tactics. Winners aren't afraid to mention the competition. It's an all-out war in nearly every American industry. Remember the "burger" wars with "Where's the beef?" and the long-distance wars in which MCI boldly states, "We save you 50 percent over AT&T"? Today, you see Coke cans in Pepsi commercials, or you hear VISA proudly stating "they don't take American Express" at the Olympics! Competition is everywhere.

If you've got competition, don't let it be an excuse not to "do it." Be thankful for it! Use the competition for all it's worth. Use it to fire up the people who work for you. Get a battle going if you have to. Take a cue from us. Most companies have a boardroom, but A. L. Williams has a war room.

Use competition to get you out doing the things that you have backed away from because you were afraid to or too lazy to do. Your competition will help you "do it"!

Learn to Deal with Fear

As amazing as it may seem from my perspective, competition is one reason people don't even try to "do it." But there's another reason. You'll never hear this reason mentioned as an excuse because no one likes to admit to it. But nine out of ten times you hear an excuse, you can bet *this* is the real reason: fear.

Let me tell you some things about fear.

Fear paralyzes.

Fear takes up all of your energy. It drains your batteries. It consumes you, and even when you're doing something you like to do, the fear of what you are putting off is alway there in the back of your mind. It destroys everything in its path. No matter how hard you try to forget about it, if you're afraid to do something like call a client or a prospect or even your boss, you won't be able to perform one other constructive act until you eliminate your fear.

Chuck Noll is a former NFL linebacker and now the coach of the four-time Super Bowl champion Pittsburgh Steelers. Noll describes fear this way: "Fear of failure can restrict a player; it can kill him as an individual. If one continually worries about failing, he'll get so tight that he will fail. . . . We want to be properly prepared for anything in a game, but we don't want to worry about losing the game."

Fear creates imaginary difficulties.

When I signed my first coaching contract, I was so thrilled. It was what I had been preparing to do for years. But you know what? That was the most intimidating thing I ever did. I was married with two kids, and I had just signed a contract to coach. The "enemy" in my mind took over. I said to myself, "Art, are you good enough? Are you sure you can cut the mustard? What if you go over there and lose? What if you go over there and you're just an average coach?"

I imagined all kinds of scenes where I'd be humiliated and run out of town. In some, we'd lose every single game. I'd get fired. I was creating all kinds of imaginary difficulties when I hadn't actually experienced a single problem.

Fear spreads like a disease.

Fear feeds on itself and multiplies. When you're afraid to tackle something, everyone knows it. The people who work for you and with you sense it, and they become alert to a new problem. They see you as their leader, and they figure that if you're afraid of something, there's a good chance it's something they should be afraid of, too.

UNWRITTEN LAW: *A leader can never show fear, never show hurt, never show quit.*

I'm not trying to scare you. That's not my intent. But I want you to see that fear will keep you from "doing it." But, folks, as strange as it may sound, the only way to eliminate fear is to "do it."

I talked in the last chapter about Bobby Buisson, the former basketball coach who refused to quit until he was successful. Bobby will tell you that his biggest problem starting out was not lack of knowledge about the business, but his inability to get started. He just couldn't for the life of him make himself "do it." It all stemmed from fear. Fear of rejection. Fear of failure.

There was a single day, however, in Bobby's career that helped him turn everything around. Bobby had recruited a guy who had just moved to Atlanta from New York. He knew no one in town and had no leads to start with. He was a lot worse off than Bobby! After hanging around the office for a few days, this guy walked into Bobby's office and said, "Bobby, I've been talking to people around here, and it looks like you can take brochures down the street and introduce yourself to people. It looks like that may be the way for me to start. Will you come with me tomorrow?"

It was like a knife through Bobby's stomach. He was the leader, and his new recruit was asking him to go with him to do what he feared most, prospecting. His reaction was immediate: "I'd love to, but I'm booked solid for the next four months."

Bobby went home that night and couldn't sleep. He kept

saying to himself, "Bobby, you chicken. Here is a guy who wants to get into the business and asks for your help, and you are so scared of going out and talking to people that you won't go with him."

Bobby decided that night that if he was going to be any kind of leader, he was going to have to set the example. If this guy's only option was to introduce himself to people, Bobby was going to have to experience this form of prospecting himself to be able to help his recruit. He decided he would get up Saturday morning and go door-to-door. So the problem was resolved, and Bobby went to sleep.

But the next Saturday, guess what happened? Bobby found an excuse and didn't go. In fact, Bobby made excuses for four more Saturdays, and the whole time, it just gnawed away at him. Finally, Bobby got up one Saturday morning, put on a suit, and told his wife he would be gone until noon.

He got into his car, drove around a couple of neighborhoods, and finally forced himself to park the car. A man opened the door at the first house he walked up to, and Bobby had no idea what to say. He was scared to death. He pulled out his business card and said, "Excuse me, my name is Bob Buisson, and I'm a neighbor of yours. I live down the street. I don't want to disturb you on a Saturday morning. I just dropped by to give you my business card." He spoke for thirty seconds straight without taking a breath. At the end, the man took his card and thanked him.

So Bobby went to the next door. He knocked on sixty-eight doors that day. At five or six houses, no one was home. He had fifteen people tell him to give them a call any time. He had five people set up definite appointments.

He had one person the whole day who was mildly nasty to him. He walked up to a house and knocked on the door and this woman opened it and Bobby said, "Ma'am, my name is Bob Buisson, and I'm a neighbor of yours . . ."

And the woman said, "Stop right there. I don't believe in door-to-door salesmen."

And Bobby said, "You better believe in this one, because here he is."

She said, "That's not what I mean."

And she slammed the door in his face and hurt his feelings.

It took him twenty-two seconds to get to the next house, and the people there were nice. In fact, people were so nice that Bobby actually began to enjoy what he was doing. Some people wanted to talk for so long that he had trouble getting away from them.

I'm not telling this story to get people who are in sales to go out and knock door-to-door. I've never believed in building a client base that way because I don't appreciate cold callers.

But the point I am making is that Bobby took action. He forced himself to do something he was afraid of. And even though he never used this method again, he had taken a tremendous step toward overcoming his fear of getting started.

In *Think and Grow Rich,* Napoleon Hill said, "Do the things you fear, and the death of fear is certain."

Folks, I believe that with everything that's in me. If there's something you're afraid to tackle that you are certain would help you get started in changing your life, go "do it."

Make a list right now of the ten things you want to do the least, but ten things that will help your business, and then do them. Once you get started, once you check those first couple of items off your list, you'll be making progress toward turning things around. You'll have shown yourself that you can "do it."

While you're "doing it," click the "off" switch on your imagination. Instead, replace it with the positive image of yourself. Think of your strengths, the things you're good at. Don't worry about things that haven't happened.

Beaten Paths Are for Beaten Men

Sometimes, the one thing that will help you become a winner is not something you dread doing or don't want to do, but something that you are just dying to do—but you don't have the courage to try. You can't bring yourself to take that big a risk. Well, folks, I believe the real winners are people who at some critical point took an important risk. Not a foolish risk, but a risk that had been carefully thought out and calculated. A risk in which the person knew the down side as well as the good side of the results of the action.

If you expect to do something really special in your life by just following what other people have already done, you can forget about "being somebody." The losers of the world are content to travel on the beaten path. Their main distinction is that they're *exactly like everybody else.* That's how they're comfortable.

Winners have something extra that makes them lie awake at night dreaming of something different, something *better.*

I found a little poem about risk in a book about sports. It has a lot to say, and it's worth sticking up on your bulletin board and looking at when you feel like running back to the safety and security of the "beaten path."

RISKS

To laugh is to risk appearing the fool.

To weep is to risk appearing sentimental.

To reach out for another is to risk involvement.

To expose feelings is to risk exposing your true self.

To place your ideas, your dreams before a crowd is to risk their loss.

To love is to risk not being loved in return.

To live is to risk dying.

To hope is to risk despair.

To try is to risk failure.

But risks must be taken, because the greatest hazard in life is to risk nothing.

The person who risks nothing, does nothing, has nothing, and is nothing.

They may avoid suffering and sorrow, but they cannot learn, feel, change, grow, love, live.

Chained by their attitudes, they are a slave, they have forfeited their freedom.

Only the person who risks is free.

—Anonymous

A guy named Frederick Wilcox once said that "progress

always involves risk; you can't steal second base and keep your foot on first." It's true. You can't *almost* take a risk. You can't hang on to your security and take a risk at the same time. Just this once, go for it. You might be surprised.

When I talk about risk (and about "doing it"), I always think of my great friend, Ginny Carter. When I try to introduce her on stage, Ginny's one of those people who just brings up emotion in me.

Ginny was probably in her late fifties when she came with me. She was raising four children by herself. Now, this business was tough on me because when I took a risk and went into business, I was scared. But my wife, Angela, was a schoolteacher, with a regular income, so at least we knew we could eat and put a roof over our heads while the business was getting started.

But Ginny was the sole provider for four children. She wasn't in a position to take a big risk. She had a pretty good job and a pretty secure position at her old company.

It was a risky proposition to come with a company that was, at that time, nothing more than an idea in my head. But Ginny came into it with her eyes open. She had heard me say that our chances of survival were slim. She had heard me tell everyone over and over again that the only way we would make it was if we would be able to "hang tough."

But Ginny took that risk. She believed in what I wanted to do, and she was willing to go for it for the opportunity to give her family a better life—if it worked out—and there were no guarantees.

Ginny had to go out and dig just like I did, but without any help or any security at all, knowing those kids were depending on her. I used to sit there in total amazement at how she did it. She made a total commitment. She said that nobody was going to deny her an opportunity, and she just did it. She had nothing but desire and a will to win.

Ginny's kids are grown now; she's put them through college and provided for them a hundred times better than most people are able to do for their kids. In fact, because of her financial position, she's been able to give her family and future generations options that they never would have had—all because she had the courage to try.

Do's for "Doing it"

Here are some points that I hope will help you today when you put down this book and go "do it":

1. DO *adopt the "little bit more" principle.*

The people who made the most money worked hard . . . *and a little bit more.* They paid the price . . . *and a little bit more.* They had determination . . . *and a little bit more.* They were committed . . . *and a little bit more.*

They were good people . . . *and a little bit more.*

Pete Rose, the great major-league first baseman, wasn't a great hitter; he wasn't a great runner or even a great fielder. But Pete Rose was a *great* baseball player. Rose understood the "little bit more" principle.

"You have to give 110 percent at anything you do," Rose said. "Because if you only give 100 percent, the guy you're playing against might be giving 100 percent and it's going to be a standoff. If you give that extra 10 percent, you've got a chance to win."

2. DO *pick one thing to go for.*

You can't do everything. You can't be great in every single area. So many people get interested in one thing and try for a little while. When it doesn't work out or they get bored, they quit and move on to a new area.

The best way you can go for it is to pick one thing and make it your life's work. Give it 110 percent, and simply refuse to admit the possibility of defeat.

UNWRITTEN LAW: *You don't have just one chance to win, but you don't have unlimited opportunities, either.*

You have to pick one option, commit to it, and don't pass it up just because the grass looks greener on the other side. Which opportunity will the next one be? Your *first,* or your *last?*

3. DO *learn to be flexible.*

In business, the rules of winning can change overnight. The businesses of the future—and the people running them— have got to be flexible, able to adjust to change.

UNWRITTEN LAW: *The only way to grow is to accept change.*

Sony is a great company that forgot to follow this rule. It was one of the first makers of home video machines, the Betamax. For a couple of years, everything in the video market was produced to fit the Beta. Then along came some other enterprising companies that developed VHS. Those took off like a rocket, and consumers seemed to like VHS better. After a while, you could hardly find any videos to fit the Beta. But Sony refused to give up on its idea. Convinced that Beta was the best system, management refused to make a VHS, even though every other company was making them and all the video stores were carrying VHS. Sony just kept making Betas.

Finally, somebody woke up and made the decision to produce the VHS machine at Sony. In the meantime, Sony had lost probably millions of dollars in sales to the other companies.

You've got to learn to roll with the punches, listen to your common sense, and always be prepared to make adjustments if the situation calls for it.

4. DO *find yourself a hero.*

Everybody needs some inspiration from time to time. When you're discouraged and down in the dumps, read about your hero. It will help to remind you that all great people had some big setbacks, but they didn't stop pursuing their dreams.

During two of the most important years of my business

life, at the point where it was really critical for me to hang tough, I'd go to the library once a quarter and check out a biography on one of my heroes. I read about The Bear, Patton, Winston Churchill, Vince Lombardi, Stonewall Jackson, and others who started out as someone average and ordinary just like me, but who went on to be something great. It was an inspiring exercise.

Find yourself a hero, and let that person be your inspiration to "do it."

5. DO *always play scared.*

Playing scared is different from *being* scared. If you play scared, you keep an eye out for what could go wrong.

UNWRITTEN LAW: *If you ever need one thing to guarantee your success, it will never happen.*

Follow the "numbers game" principle: the only way to keep from losing is to have a number of possibilities.

I just can't understand it when people try to qualify for a promotion by making the exact number of sales required. Then, when one sale falls through for one reason or another, they've lost. Playing scared means never cutting it that close. If you need ten sales to make your income goal, make fifteen or twenty. Playing scared means socking money away when things are going good, just in case you have a slump. It means working like today might be your last chance, even if you know it isn't. Be positive, but recognize that "gotchas" pop up when and where you least expect them. If you don't play scared, you'll get caught.

Nothing Great Comes without a Price

One final note. Don't sit around waiting. I promise that *you don't get something for nothing in this world.* Decide on the price you are willing to pay for success.

As I go around the country, I always talk about how great it is to win. But it's really something you can't explain. It's like talking in a foreign language. People just can't identify with what you're saying.

Everyone would love it if I sat down with our lawyers and had them draw up a contract that gave a guaranteed income of $100,000 a year. That's what professional athletes want. They want a guaranteed contract that will pay them, whether they play or not. But it doesn't work that way in the real world. There are no guarantees. You're going to have to pay a price to win.

But winners, when they finally "make it" and see how great it is, always look back at the price they paid and say, "As great as I thought it would be to win, this is a thousand times better. I'd pay that same price double again."

You know when you really understand how great it is to win? When you win. Only then do you know. And then the price you paid seems small and insignificant.

If Bobby knew when he first started out prospecting that day, going door-to-door, that someday he was going to be financially independent, do you think he would do it again? Of course he would! He'd do it a hundred times again. That's how great the reward is.

You're going to have to pay a price. You know that. You don't know how great a price, but you do know that as long as you don't quit and give up, you'll succeed. Once you realize this, why don't you go "do it"? Get started now. Get over that first hurdle of inactivity.

Don't spend your life just dreaming about "doing it." A lot of people will *try* to "do it." A lot of people will *want* to "do it." A lot of people will *almost* "do it."

But winners *will* "do it."

What do they do?

They do whatever it takes to get the job done.

You may be saying, "But, Art, I don't know what to do!"

"Fine, just do it."

"Art, I'm scared to death every day."

"OK, just do it."

"Art, I want to be somebody so bad I can't stand it."
"Super. Just do it."
"Art, I'm afraid I'm going to fail."
"Great! Just do it."
"Art, I don't know if I know how to compete anymore."
"I understand. Just do it."
"Art, I don't know if I can pay the price."
"Just do it."
"Art, I'm not making any money. What do I do?"
"You just do it."
"Art, if I could just pay off this debt."
"Right. Just do it."
"Art, I don't know if I can keep on keeping on. What now?"
"Just do it and do it and do it."
"Art, if I could sell my house and get on my feet."
"Sounds good, do it."
"But houses aren't selling right now."
"Fine. Do it anyway."
"Art, I'm going to start saving money so I'll never have to go through this again."
"Great. Do it!"
"Art, do you mean that somebody that looks like me has gotta do it?"
"Yeah, you really gotta do it."
"Do *what*, Art?"
"You just do it, and then do it some more."
"Art, if I could just learn to take a risk."
"Do it."
"But I've never taken a risk before!"
"Do it anyway."
"Art, I'm really hurting."
"Then go do it!"
"Art, what do I do during the tough times?"
"You just do it
    and do it,
    and do it,
    and do it,
    until you win."

CHAPTER TWELVE

Warning: Don't Blow It

Better is little with the fear of the Lord, than great treasure, and trouble therewith.

Ben Franklin

Now, take a "time-out" with me one more time before you start on the road to your personal dream of success. Let's say you reach your goals; you get all the success and achievement and recognition from your working life that you've ever wanted.

But wait.

You can have all the success in the world and make all the money in the world, but if you don't have your priorities straight, you're going to be a failure. If you don't win in *all areas of your life,* you're ultimately a *loser.*

Other people may look at you and say, "Man, that guy's got all this money, all this fame and fortune, all this power. He's got everything!" But you're still your toughest critic—and the only true critic. If you look at yourself in the mirror and say, "Man, you're the biggest loser that's ever been. How did you mess up your life so bad?" you haven't made a success of your life.

There's so much more to life than winning in business. Don't tell me that you're a winner if you've made a lot of money, but failed in your personal life—with your spouse, your kids, or your other personal relationships.

The best example I know is a guy named Boe Adams. In everybody's eyes, he was a hero. But he blew it. I was reluctant to tell Boe's story because people can be cruel and the memories are still painful for him and his family. But I am telling it because it's a graphic example of what can happen when you get sidetracked into thinking business success is the only thing that matters and because it's an exciting story of recovery and rebirth.

Blowing It—and Coming Back

Boe Adams is one of my closest personal friends and a business associate of many years. Boe grew up poor in a family of twelve in Leachville, Arkansas. He was six feet five and light on his feet, and he got his first taste of success in high school on the basketball court. When he discovered his skill at basketball, he threw himself into the game. Every night after school, he'd shoot baskets until dark. It paid off; Boe was good enough to be recruited by many major colleges.

Boe was one of those rare people who seemed to have an inborn discipline. He excelled at whatever he put his mind to. When he graduated from college, he went to work as a basketball coach. Then he started selling life insurance part-time, and he did so well that he gave up his coaching job and went full-time.

By the time he was in his late twenties, Boe had hit it big. He moved to Texas to help start a new insurance company. Before he was thirty, Boe was running the company. His life seemed like a storybook tale; he was a multimillionaire, president of a large company. He was inducted into his university's Hall of Distinction, and his hometown of Leachville proclaimed a Boe Adams Day, the only time that honor was ever bestowed. He had a beautiful wife and five children. He traveled in private jets and rubbed elbows with people in high places. People looked at Boe with awe. For a boy from Arkansas, it was pretty heady stuff.

Then something happened to demolish his dreams. Somewhere along the way, Boe had gotten his priorities mixed up. His desire for success had overshadowed other areas of his life. In his zeal to "be somebody," Boe had gotten in over his head. He was running with a freewheeling crowd. For them, deals and deal making were par for the course. His so-called friends advised him of shortcuts that were lucrative, but not quite legal. Boe knew that what he was doing was funny business, but his friends assured him that "everybody did it."

Suddenly, everything blew up in Boe's face. He discovered that the fancy maneuvering that "everybody did" was called securities fraud by the federal authorities. In a whirl of confusion and regret, Boe's life was destroyed. The status, the power, the money—everything disappeared overnight. Within a few months, he was completely broke, his family life was shattered, and he faced twelve months in a minimum-security prison for the securities violations. The dream turned into a nightmare.

Boe lost his fortune and his status, and he almost lost his family. He was totally devastated. The heartbreak and suffering were almost unbearable. All the friends and advisers disappeared, and Boe was left alone with his mistake.

For most people, it would have been the end of the line. Any hopes he might have had for success were dashed forever— or so it seemed.

But Boe wasn't an ordinary person. He was an exceptional person who had "blown it" in a big way, but he was a survivor. During this period, Boe had a lot of time to think about his mistakes. He rediscovered the Bible, and during those twelve months, he read it, cover to cover, three times. The lessons he learned there gave him the ability—and the strength—to turn his life around.

Then Boe started over. After regaining his spiritual life, he started repairing the damage to his family. With those two powers behind him, Boe started over with a vengeance. He held his head up high, and he never looked back. He made up his mind that even though he had made a terrible mistake, he had paid dearly for it. He would not let it defeat him.

Boe went back to the area he knew best—insurance—and

worked like never before. Whenever he saw a better opportunity, he jumped for it. People had to acknowledge that Boe was a maniac on the job, giving 150 percent every day.

When I first met Boe in 1977, I knew I had met someone special. His insurance knowledge and management abilities were just extraordinary. I sensed I had met a genius. I asked him to work as a consultant for the company we had started. We were pretty tiny back then, with not much more than a good idea and a lot of heart. I figured if Boe was willing to take a chance on us, I was willing to take one on him. It was a bet I won over and over again as Boe proved invaluable to the little company that didn't stay little for very long.

I knew Boe was a brilliant man, but at a critical time in our company he proved his heart as well. Things were going well, but we wanted to create a new position in our company that would give our salespeople a new challenge to reach for. The problem was, we couldn't afford to do it. We just didn't have the money. We felt the company was ready to take off, and this position would give us the boost we needed for our people.

Boe came to me one day and said, "Art, A. L. Williams has a chance to do something historic in American business, and I want to be a part of it. I want to make a difference. I blew it one time in my life, and I just want to go out a winner." Boe wasn't financially independent in those days, and he had a family to support. But that day, Boe gave up half his consulting income so I could fund the position the company needed.

As it turned out, our company boomed, and Boe made back that income many times over. But when he made that sacrifice, it was far from a sure thing. Fifteen years after his devastation, Boe is ten times the success that he was in those early years. He came back bigger and better than ever. He's a multimillionaire who has been instrumental in A. L. Williams's success. Boe has also touched the lives of hundreds of thousands of people across the U.S.; his personal example has motivated thousands who had given up on their lives because success seemed too difficult.

Over the years, Boe has told me many times that he would

gladly give up all his wealth and possessions before he would hurt his reputation and his family again.

"Don't Blow It" Warning #1: *Don't compromise your integrity.*

You may not be in a disaster stage, but you can still be in danger of blowing it. You don't have to blow it in a million-dollar way like Boe Adams did to be in danger. Everyone faces temptations every day in small ways that call for compromises.

It's easy to pass off the "little lie" or the "small accounting procedure" when it would help you out or work toward your benefit. You can say, "Nobody will know. Everybody does it." Right?

Wrong!

One time in particular, we were lobbying to defeat a bill in our state legislature that we felt would deal a death blow to our young company. I met with a couple of legislators in a motel room, just like in the movies. They told me if I would give them $10,000 or $15,000, they could get the bill killed. I was tempted, but I knew in my heart that this was wrong. I decided that if that was what it took to win, I didn't want any part of it. I didn't want to compete that way; I wanted our company to win the *right* way. Things did work out in our favor, and the bill never passed. I might have paid off those politicians and no one would have ever known, but I would have set a pattern for operating the business that would have ultimately destroyed it.

I take a hard line at A. L. Williams on honesty and integrity issues. I'll terminate a person ten times more quickly for an action that involves a lack of decency and integrity than for a mistake that costs the company a lot of money.

"Don't Blow It" Warning #2: *Handle your money wisely.*

Another way I've seen people blow their opportunity to be successful and make a difference with their lives is by mismanaging and misusing their money. It doesn't matter whether your income is modest or substantial, it's important to be a good steward of whatever money you have. If you aren't wise, if you aren't conservative in this area, you'll blow it.

One rule we always live by is to "be lean and mean." I believe that most people who go into business for themselves fail because they don't have enough cash flow to survive. They're always doing dumb things—investing too much money back into their business or simply raising their standard of living too high. They think the money's always going to come in and they're always going to grow.

But remember my unwritten law that the first eighteen months in business, everything turns into a mess? That's the catch. Businesses don't usually grow at a level pace. The first three to five years in business you're on a roller coaster. Every time you get something going you're going to have a reversal.

The important thing is to have the ability to survive when times get tough and the income stops flowing for a while. You've got to be liquid, with plenty of cash on hand for the inevitable emergencies.

Here's a hint to tell you if you're on the right track in your business or career. If the people around you don't say you're cheap or accuse you of being a miser (at least in a joking way), you're probably not running the finances of your business the right way.

UNWRITTEN LAW:	*It's not how much you earn; it's how much you keep that counts.*

Don't misunderstand me. I'm not saying you should have a goal of accumulating and counting money and just being miserly. Those people with significant amounts of money have a great obligation to make a difference in the world by giving it back to help their fellow human beings. However, only those who can make money and save it are able to give—to their family, to those around them, to their community. A lot of people in this country are making money and throwing it away. In my opinion, they are blowing it.

These days, there are a lot of advocates of the "fake it till you make it" theory. It goes like this: if you're not making it, go out and buy a big car, move into a big house, have a big office. Look successful, even though you aren't. Successful people will be attracted to you; you'll move in all the "right circles." Image is everything.

Wrong again.

I ran smack into that theory with a friend of mine from the company. I went to visit his office in Portland, Maine, and he met me at the airport in a big Mercedes. We pulled up to a beautiful office complex, with three more Mercedes parked out front. I knew these people weren't making that kind of money yet, and I asked him about it. He explained that he and his group were trying to "show success" to the community; they believed that kind of "implied success" would create clients.

That's superficial and artificial, and it won't work. People may buy it at first, but sooner or later, they're going to find you out. Plus, spending your valuable time concocting plans like that is a waste of effort (not to mention a huge waste of money). People should come to you because what you're doing is right and good for them, not because you have the biggest car or the most impressive office or the most expensive clothes.

I drove used cars long after I had a lot of money saved. I operated out of small offices; I never wore expensive clothes. When I was selling insurance and investments part-time, I saved all my money. Then rather than show off a big car and a big house and all that other paraphernalia, I showed my personal investments to people. After two and a half years of selling part-time, I had $42,000 in my investment program. Showing people how I had saved that money with my part-time job and built it up over that time period was a much bigger statement of what I was doing than a car or house.

Even though I never made over $35,000 a year my first six years in the insurance business, after just six years, Angela and I had saved $100,000. We were tough on ourselves because we had a goal. We lived well below our means, spending only what we could afford from my coaching salary and saving the money

I made from my part-time job. This enabled us to keep our business moving forward.

UNWRITTEN LAW: *Watch your pennies, and your dollars will take care of themselves.*

You know, people want to snap their fingers and be millionaires overnight. That's not the way it works. To accumulate $1 million, you've got to first save $1, then $100, then $1,000, then $10,000 and $20,000 and so on. That's how you build it up, by saving that first dollar.

Panic or Peace of Mind?

Building up an emergency fund can make the difference between panic and peace of mind. You should always have an emergency fund equal to three to six months' income. Then when things get tight, you don't have to put your business on hold because there's no money.

The bigger your income gets, the bigger your emergency fund should be. When you're making a big income, you should have a fund equal to two or three years' income.

The $42,000 that Angela and I saved when I was part-time gave us the "comfort zone" to go full-time. We never touched that money, but we always knew it was there if we needed it, that we could live on that for a couple of years if we had to. By the time we started A. L. Williams, Angela and I had accumulated $200,000 in cash, mainly from my part-time income selling insurance and investments. We put that $200,000 up and said, "We're willing to invest this in our new business to see if we can really achieve our dreams." That money kept our business going. When we got into nearly impossible situations or frustrating situations, we didn't have to panic financially. You just can't measure that kind of security when you're launching a new career or business.

| UNWRITTEN LAW: | *Always live below your means.* |

A lot of people tell you to live *within* your means. I think that's a big mistake. If you're trying to reach a special goal, like my goal of financial independence, you've got to live *below* your means.

I set some guidelines for myself when I set out to become financially independent, and they worked like a charm for me and my family.

I decided to *save 50 percent of every paycheck.* Unthinkable? No. You can do it if you're serious about your goals and willing to live below your means.

As our income improved, I wanted to improve our lifestyle, but decided to *wait two years* before making changes. With most people, the first month they have a big increase in income, they go out and buy a big house, a boat, a vacation home, or some other luxury. Don't do it! You're not allowing for those lows that are bound to come. Once you hit a steady level of earnings and you really begin to see bigger success than you've had in the past, wait two years. Don't spend. Just double or triple on your investment program. The payoff will be a lot greater in the long run.

I decided to *start saving now.* Don't procrastinate about beginning a serious savings program. If you start now, you're far ahead of the game. Waiting *hurts.* Let me show you why.

If you began saving $1 a day, invested at 12 percent (compounded annually until age sixty-five):

		Total at age 65	*Cost to Wait*
Begin saving:	*Age 25*	$296,516	$ ---
	Age 26	264,404	32,114
	Age 30	116,858	179,658

If you're age twenty-five and you postpone saving for just *one year,* you lose $32,114. If you postpone five years—only five!—

you lose an amazing $179,658. Time and consistency are the keys to building security in your financial future. Don't delay!

Decide to *pay one price*. Most people pay a series of prices in their life. They work hard and make money for two or three years, then they get impatient and spend money for four or five years. Then they have to start all over again. They repeat this pattern over and over. Instead of paying a series of prices, work hard for five to ten years, save your money, reach your goals, and be financially free for the rest of your life. I decided to pay my price early, to hold tough when I wanted to spend because I knew in time it would pay off.

Handling money wisely, being a good steward, being responsible, not placing value on the wrong things, being patient to let efforts compound—the *lack* of any of these things can cause you to blow it.

"Don't Blow It" Warning #3: *You can't be selfish or self-centered.*

I see so many people whose careers fall apart because they get the disease of "self-ness." I call it a disease because of the distress it causes in their lives and the lives of those around them.

Be on the lookout for the symptoms of this disease in yourself:

✔ You say "me," "my," "mine," instead of "you" or "the team."

✔ What "you" want and need dominates your thinking; you rarely think of the needs or wants of others.

✔ All of your efforts are directed at *your* success; you've stopped helping other people achieve their goals.

✔ You see the success of others as a threat to your own success.

If you recognize any of these symptoms in yourself, take some time out and think about what I call the "giving principle of life."

UNWRITTEN LAW: *Most people fail because they lose sight of the "giving principle of life."*

The heart of the giving principle is the Bible. In the sixth chapter of Luke, it says, "Give, and it will be given to you" (verse 38). If you don't give to others in all areas of your life, including your business life, you won't continue to grow and develop.

People need other people. One of the funny things about giving is that the more you give, the more you receive.

✔   The more you help others, the greater your own success will be.

✔   The more love and support you give, the more you'll get back.

✔   The more you focus on helping people through your business, the bigger your business will grow.

Some people may say, "Art, come on. That 'give, and it will be given' stuff is for Sunday school. It doesn't hold up in the dog-eat-dog world of business."

Wrong! So many people start out in business to just help themselves; it never works. The businesses that grow and prosper are the businesses that produce a product or provide a service to help people or improve their lives. That's a fact.

You can get by on selfishness for a while. Some people and companies have built fortunes on it. But it rarely lasts.

Follow the giving principle in your business life. Make giving to others a way of life. It's not just about religion. It's about feeling good about people and, as a bonus, feeling good about yourself and your life.

"Don't Blow It" Warning #4: *Have the right priorities.*

Truly successful people know the secret of living a balanced life. They manage to strike a critical balance between their business life, their personal life, and their spiritual life.

But they must also include themselves in there somewhere. People who neglect themselves in their efforts to win will probably suffer great health problems or severe mental and emotional problems.

A healthy body is one of life's most precious possessions. It's so easy to ignore our health; but without good health, the other blessings of life can't be enjoyed to their fullest.

The health trend today is one of the best things that's happening in our country. Bookstores and television shows are filled with good information on how to get healthy and stay healthy. I know you're saying, "Art, I don't have time for all that exercise stuff." Please take time. You can't afford *not* to. When you abuse your body, everyone around you suffers because you aren't your best.

I believe the right priorities are God first, family second, and business third. You can't just say that; you have to live it.

It always breaks my heart to see people in business who believe that the way to succeed is to put 100 percent of their effort into their business and neglect their family. The divorce rate in America is 50 percent today. But I heard on television the other day that for executives earning more than $50,000, that rate is a staggering 85 percent.

Those people may succeed in their business life, but they'll wake up one day to discover that a business is all they have. So many people realize, too late, that no life based on business success alone is a happy life.

Family

So many business executives take their families for granted only to discover the heartaches of what happens when family takes a backseat to business.

Folks, you know deep down what your family means to you. Don't treat it as something that will just take care of itself; it won't. Give it the same attention that you give your working life; the success won't mean much with no one to share it.

The sales business is a demanding business. At A. L. Williams, Angela and I were so concerned about providing an environment that emphasized the family that we started an organization for the spouses of our salespeople, both male and female. The Partners Organization is a way to include partners in the business lives of their spouses. Partners are always invited to meetings, conventions, conferences, or any other business functions our salespeople attend. They have their own meetings and activities as well.

A few years ago, we went one step further. Angela and I discovered a great organization in Texas called Family and Marriage Resources that had as its focus promoting healthy family life. We invited that organization into our company to help our people in whatever way was needed. Today, Family and Marriage Resources conducts marriage and family seminars and programs at every A. L. Williams convention. In addition, these people travel across the country, holding special meetings with our people in groups and providing one-on-one counseling to couples who request it. To date, introducing this program to the company has been one of our proudest accomplishments. I can't tell you how Angela and I felt recently when a couple in the company sent me their divorce papers in the mail, torn in half, with a note of thanks for the help they had received and the company's commitment to families.

I can't overemphasize the importance of keeping your priorities straight. I know it's easy to say and terribly hard to do. Understand that you'll mess up every day. But you've got to keep trying. If you don't grow in all areas, you're going to wind up blowing your business and being a broken, unhappy person. The people I know who have succeeded greatly will quickly tell you that they have improved in *all areas* of their lives.

Spiritual

As they become successful, a lot of people get the idea that they don't need anything except themselves. People can easily become too materialistic, worshiping their accomplishments instead of God. They see the results of their achievements or their efforts and take the credit rather than give that credit to God. And they become egotistical instead of humble.

It's easy to blow it where your spiritual life is concerned. God should come first, and that relationship should permeate every other area of your life.

If you let your spiritual life take a backseat to everything else, if you let your spiritual life fall apart, you're denying yourself the inner peace and strength that can carry you through the tough times in your life.

I'm a Christian, and I try daily to keep Christ the center of my life and to submit to Him as Lord in my life. It's a walk in faith that is increased through Bible reading and prayer. My spiritual life is based on my relationship with God through Jesus Christ. Knowing He's always there to strengthen me, I know that I can do "all things" just as the apostle Paul wrote almost two thousand years ago. That's having a built-in success principle that can't be defeated. The whole world can be against me, but as one of my former ministers loved to say, "Me and God always make a majority."

Ultimately, I know that God is in control. He's the master architect. His plan and purpose for my life is and always will be the best.

I must be honest and say that at times with my human understanding of events, I couldn't see anything good on the horizon. For example, the small company that first underwrote our insurance business ran out of money within six months. At that same time, our state legislature had a bill that, if passed, would have destroyed our business. That was a disastrous time for us. But in the midst of this I met Boe Adams, and he introduced us to a larger company with greater resources. A couple of years later, the owner of that company died suddenly, and the company was going to be sold. That was another crisis, and we were forced to go with another company, one that built an administrative facility in the Atlanta area, which was something we desperately needed.

Even when disasters came, I see now how much God was

in control. He was closing one door in order to open another. I was forced to face a major challenge in order to grow or change in some area of my life.

I know that God wants my best. I know I'm supposed to show up and try each day to get better. He supplies the power that adds a strength I can't supply. In the Bible, He's given me all the principles I need for life. If I follow those principles, I'll be in His will and purpose for my life.

In our business life, I've prayed daily for God to bless the efforts of the people in our company and to make our goals ones that would please Him. I want our goal to be more than just helping people create financial independence. I have an equally important goal of helping them to become more fulfilled individuals in all areas of their lives.

Don't let yourself fall into the pattern of thinking that God is just for Sunday. Remember right and wrong. Remember your spiritual life. The rewards are tremendous.

I encourage you to put the highest priority on your spiritual life. As a businessperson, you'll face a lot of tough choices and tough decisions. Without that foundation to give you strength, to provide inner peace, and to help you make the right choices, both you and your business will eventually suffer.

Glenn Bland in his book *Success,* published fifteen years ago, gives the best example I've ever seen of the importance of priorities. It shows vividly that success and money alone can't buy happiness and peace of mind.

Bland tells of a meeting in 1923 of the world's most successful financiers held at Chicago's Edgewater Beach Hotel. In terms of money, these financial giants almost literally ruled the world. Look at their names and positions: *Charles Schwab,* the president of the largest steel company in America; *Samuel Insull,* president of the largest utility company; *Howard Hopson,* president of the largest gas company; *Arthur Cutten,* the greatest wheat speculator; *Richard Whitney,* president of the New York Stock Exchange; *Albert Fall,* the secretary of the interior in President Harding's cabinet; *Jesse Livermore,* the greatest "bear" on Wall Street; *Ivar Kreuger,* head of the world's greatest monopoly;

Leon Fraser, president of the Bank of International Settlements.

These men were "movers and shakers," the kind of people we envy and wish we could be like. Yet something went terribly wrong with their lives. Twenty-five years later, look where they were:

✔ Charles Schwab went bankrupt and lived the last five years of his life on borrowed money.
✔ Samuel Insull died in a foreign land, a fugitive from justice, penniless.
✔ Howard Hopson was insane.
✔ Arthur Cutten became insolvent and died abroad.
✔ Richard Whitney had just been released from Sing Sing prison.
✔ Albert Fall had been pardoned from prison and died at home—broke.
✔ Jesse Livermore committed suicide.
✔ Ivar Kreuger committed suicide.
✔ Leon Fraser committed suicide.

Do you still wish you could be like these people? They had everything money could buy, all the success they could ever desire. But they're a testament to the fact that business success alone isn't enough.

It's a sobering story, but there's a great message. Don't blow it! Be "lean and mean," don't give in to "self-ness," and have the right priorities.

Your life from this moment forward is a blank page. Fill it with the richness of spiritual fulfillment, family joy, and a healthy body and mind, and your goals and dreams of success will be a hundred times more exciting and enjoyable when you reach them.

All You Can Do Is All You Can Do

All you can do is all you can do, but all you can do is enough.

Art Williams

A re you ready to "do it"? Now you've got the keys, at least as I've experienced them in my career in business. If you use them and take this message to heart, I don't just hope it will help you—I *know* it will. I've seen it work dozens, even hundreds, of times. At A. L. Williams, I've seen hundreds of people completely change the pattern of their lives just by making the decision to take charge of their own lives.

Part of this is because we built our company to avoid what we saw wrong with many big companies in America. But I believe that a lot of the success has come from taking to heart the ideas and techniques in this book. I know they will work for you, too.

Your job now is to make some tough decisions about your life. If you've gotten to this point in the book, my guess is that you're one of those people who is having trouble sleeping at night. You aren't satisfied with your life. You know you were put here to be somebody, but you just don't quite know how to get started. I hope *All You Can Do Is All You Can Do* has given you the push you needed. It's up to you to take it all the way.

The first decision you've got to make is the decision to

change. That's the toughest one of all. Are you willing to change? If you're going to win, you're going to have to change as a person. Establish different priorities in your life. Be willing to pay a price. Pick one thing to go for. Be willing to go forward with your life—not in a little way, but in a big way. Attempting to change is one of the hardest things you'll ever do; at the same time, the ability to change is the greatest gift that we have as human beings. It's tough, but God has granted us the capacity for change.

You can change your thinking from negative to positive, you can change your performance from bad to good, you can change your mind-set from mentally weak to mentally tough, and you can change from inactivity to activity.

You can change your life. And you can change it within thirty days if you really want to—starting right now.

But don't get me wrong. When I talk about change, I'm talking about improving yourself and your life. That doesn't mean that you have to go out and try to copy some other person. You can get inspiration from others, but you can't be somebody else—and you don't need to be. You be you. Don't try to be Art Williams. Don't try to be Lee Iacocca. Don't try to be your next-door neighbor.

As I've said throughout this book, to win you must do all *you* can possibly do—*you,* not someone else. You must be all you can personally be. And that will be enough.

I can't promise you instant success, and I can't promise you that you'll be a millionaire by age thirty-seven. But I think I've learned enough throughout the last twenty years to be able to make some promises about what will happen if you make that tough decision to change your life.

✔   I promise you an opportunity to dream again.
✔   I promise you a chance to hope again.
✔   I promise you an opportunity to be somebody you're proud of.
✔   I promise you a chance to be proud of yourself again and to make your family proud of you.

✔ I promise you that most people who read this book won't do it. Most of you won't win.

✔ I promise you most people won't become financially independent or successful because the price is so high.

✔ I promise you that most of you will get tired along the way. You'll want to rest, and some of you will want to give up.

✔ But I promise you that some of you won't give up.

✔ I promise you that some of you will look back on today and be amazed that you wasted so much of your life before you got serious.

✔ I promise you that some of you will look in the mirror and you'll smile at the person you see.

✔ I promise you that some of you will win.

✔ I promise you that it won't be easy.

✔ But I promise you that it will be worth it.

✔ I promise you that all you can do is all you can do, but I promise you that all you can do is enough.

You know, when I went into this business, I had just lost my dad. I saw my mom really have to suffer because my dad didn't have enough life insurance. When my cousin came along and introduced me to the term insurance concept, I got so excited, I became a real crusader. I was so committed to what I was doing, it never occurred to me that everyone else wouldn't share my enthusiasm and immediately say, "Yes! I want the insurance you're selling!" I knew I had the answer.

But you know what happened? I would go into a home and show people the concept. I was so enthusiastic, so fired up. I would work up a proposal, do a great job for people, and try to save them a ton of money. And the people would look at me across the kitchen table and say, "No!" "No, No, No." "No, thank you." "No, I don't want any." "No, I'm not interested." "NO!" And every time, I'd put that smile on my face, and I'd say everything I was supposed to. I'd say, "Well, Tom, it's been great meeting you, and I love your wife and kids. If you ever change your mind, just give me a call. If you see anyone who wants term insurance, please let me know."

And before I hit the door, my mind was racing, and I'd say to myself, "Art, you're such a dud! What's wrong with you? Why did you say that third sentence? It was so stupid. Why didn't you say this? Art, how could you mess up so bad? Why don't you admit it? People like you aren't supposed to make it. Just throw in the towel. Go on back and coach football for a living."

It was eating me up. All I heard were the "noes." They haunted me. I was miserable every time, devastated every time.

Then all of a sudden, one of my clients died, and I had to deliver a death claim to the widow. I paid a death claim for $150,000 to the widow, and had I not gone to see that family, she would have had only $22,000.

Something changed. I said, "Man, that's unbelievable. I just saved that family's life. I just kept that widow and her kids from being totally destitute."

And it hit me. All I had been *hearing* were the "noes." I started thinking about all the "yes" answers I'd gotten and how much money I'd saved people. I began to realize how much I'd helped the families I'd worked with. And I realized that just because I knew I was right, not everybody was going to see that. Not everybody was going to believe it. But that didn't mean that it wasn't right, and it didn't mean that I wasn't doing something good for people. Most important, it didn't mean I was a loser just because somebody said no.

This may not sound so profound, but it was a major event for me. It changed my whole way of thinking. From that time on, when I made a sales call, I would give my very best presentation. I would try so hard and give it everything I had. And people kept saying no. But every time I had a negative response, I'd put a smile on my face. I'd say, "Thank you, Bill, it's been good meeting you. I love your wife and kids. Blah, blah, blah, if you ever change your mind, give me a call."

I'd hit the door, and before I got outside, I'd say to myself, "You know, Art, you've analyzed hundreds of policies over the last year, and of all the bad policies you've seen, that guy's had to be the worst. But, you know, that guy is the loser, not Art Williams. He's a nice guy, and he's making a mistake, but there's nothing you can do about that now."

I kept on trucking. I began to live for the people who said yes. After years of frustration, I finally understood that no matter how hard you work, no matter how committed you are, everything isn't going to go the way you planned. Not everybody is going to buy. Your good people are going to quit. Your associates are going to disappoint you. People will deceive you. Sometimes, even your spouse will think you're nuts.

But all you can do is all you can do. Stamp those nine words into your brain. *All you can do is all you can do.*

No matter how well you are doing your job, everyone is not going to recognize it; everybody won't buy; everybody won't come to work with you; everybody won't think you're wonderful. But if they don't buy what you're selling (or doing), does that make you wrong? NO. Does that make you a loser? NO. You're still the same devoted, dedicated person you've always been. You haven't changed. You've got to learn to live for the *rightness* of what you're doing, to live for the goals you've set for you and your family. You can't live for the approval of every person you meet during your lifetime. You owe your love and loyalty to the people who believe in you, the people who are willing to work with you, the people who do believe in what you're doing.

Whatever the rest of the world is doing, you've got to stay and fight. That intangible is a major key to victory. That's one of the differences between victory and defeat. And, folks, that's all up to you.

Take Responsibility for Your Life

You will make or break your career. When you get ready to stand and fight for your future, you've got to accept responsibility. You can't pass it along to anybody else. If you decide that your life belongs to you, you can't blame others. You are responsible for the good things that happen in your life and for the bad things, too.

You know, there's nothing that wears me out more than these football coaches who get beat, and the first thing you see in the newspaper is a bunch of excuses. They blame the loss on somebody else. Good coaches are supposed to win in spite of the injuries, the bad calls, the disappointments in the first quarter, in spite of whatever happens out there. They're not supposed to win only if everything goes right, if they get all the breaks. They're supposed to win—no matter what.

UNWRITTEN LAW: *Excuses don't count.*

No matter how many times you hear "NO!" you're supposed to win anyway. You can't blame your failures on someone else or something that went wrong. You can't expect your spouse or your friends to constantly motivate you and keep you pumped up. You have to learn to take the failures and keep on trucking. *You* have to motivate you. Nobody else can. Sometimes when I speak at conventions of our company, someone will come up to me afterward and say, "Art, if I could just work around you every day, my life would be completely different."

Wrong.

It's just like the coach who tries to motivate the football team. He gets in there before the game, and he pumps his players up. He's so excited, he's so tough, and the players listen to him and can hardly sit on the benches. They want to get out there and demolish the other team.

Well, that works for a few minutes. They feel unified; they feel like a team. But you know what? I realized a long time ago that football is not really a team game. It is in one sense, because the team has to practice together and work together to make it work. But after all that is developed and after all the coach's motivational speeches have ended, football is an individual game. It's you against that guy right across from you in the different colored jersey. Somebody is going to win. And the person who wins will be the person who is just a little bit tougher, the person who wants it just a little bit more.

Let's take a "worst case." Let's say that time runs out. Maybe you don't go all the way. If you give 110 percent, like Pete Rose, and you don't hold anything back, then even if you don't make it, you'll have the satisfaction of knowing you lived your life like a winner. You'll be able to look at yourself in the mirror and say, "Man, maybe I didn't set the world on fire, but I sure did smoke it up a little bit."

There's no dishonor in failing if you truly give it everything you have. The only real disgrace is never trying. The only real heartbreak is having that desire in your heart and never putting it on the line.

I'll always remember watching the Broncos play the Redskins in the 1988 Super Bowl. John Elway played that game like he was on fire. When things started going wrong, he played even harder. It seemed like they were jinxed; nothing would work. But the worse things got, the harder Elway played. In some of the worst moments of the game, the camera would catch Elway's face, and you could see the faintest hint of a smile. The announcers couldn't believe it. How could the guy be smiling when they were down by three or four touchdowns?

I think Elway was smiling because he knew he was giving it his best shot. He was glad to have made it into the final game. He came to play, and if the plays didn't work and the receivers dropped the ball, well, that wasn't going to keep him from playing the best game he could. After that game, Elway was gracious and proud. He was the kind of player every coach wishes he had eleven of on his team. He said good things about the Broncos, and he said what a great team the Redskins had. Yeah, you could say Elway was a loser. But I don't think he was a loser, and I don't think he thought so, either.

He did his very best, and that was all he could do.

Having said all that, I really believe that nine times out of ten, all you can do is going to be enough. The world is full of people who play at half or a third of their ability. If you go out there and do all you can do, you may not win every time, but you'll win more than you lose. And when they click your lights out, you'll have been everything you ever thought you could be.

You're Here for Only a Flicker

You know, you are here on this earth for only a flicker. Just a flicker, and then it's over. I remember when my son, little Art, was born. We went back to my home to have a family picture made. My great-grandmother was still living, and little Art made five generations living in the Williams family. You know, I used to look at my mother and daddy as old people. I used to look at my grandparents as death warmed over. And I don't even know what I thought about my great-grandparents. They were so ancient they were like those mummies in the pyramids. I couldn't even picture anybody being that old.

Folks, right now in the Williams chain, I'm the oldest. I've got grandkids. Sometimes, I can't believe it. I'm forty-six years old, and I don't feel one day over sixteen. I don't have much hair, and what I've got is grey. But I still don't feel one day older than I did when I was sixteen. I still think I can do everything that I did then. I just don't know where all that time went.

I believe that time runs out for most people because they keep saying, "My time's gonna come," and all of a sudden, it's over and they didn't pick out one thing to go for. Life is just a flicker, and it's flying by. It's not waiting for some special time when it's gonna stop and be *our time.*

Many people are waiting for something special to happen. But that's just another excuse. They haven't realized that life doesn't give you what you would love to have, life doesn't give you what you want. Life gives you what you will accept.

UNWRITTEN LAW: *The world isn't going to stop and wait for you.*

It took me a long time to figure this unwritten law out. I believe the sun is gonna come up tomorrow and go down tomorrow night, and it's gonna come up the next day and go down the next night. Isn't that revolutionary? Isn't that amazing? But so many times, we don't realize that.

You know how I figured that out? Because I kept waking up every day thinking the world was going to pieces. I'm a big history nut. I like to go back and look at the problems we've faced in the past. And you know what I've found? They're no different from the problems we face today. There have been a lot of times in the United States when people thought there was no reason for hope. But the sun came up the next day and on and on.

The one thing you can count on is that time just keeps on going. Let me give you another unwritten law.

UNWRITTEN LAW: *Things are about like they always have been.*

How about that? And things in the future will be like they always have been. You see, you and I are just going to be here for a flicker. The United States is going to be here way after we're gone, right? I don't know any quicker way to fail than to worry about how the world is going to pieces and the economy is bad and things are worse than they've ever been, and so on and so on. You turn on the news for thirty minutes, and when you turn it off, you're just so depressed you can hardly stand it. You think things are bad all over. Everybody is getting beaten. The world is too tough a place to make a difference in.

But we're just here for a flicker. I don't know if we're going to have a war, but I'm not going to sit in my easy chair and worry about it. I don't know if somebody's going to drop a bomb on us, but I'm not going to put my life on hold waiting to find out. It's just a flicker, right?

Take time to focus on you and your place in the world just the way it is.

The Person in the Mirror

You can't avoid him.
You can't ever get away from him.
Every day you have to report to him.
At the end of your life, he'll be there.
No one else can see him.
No one else matters quite as much.

That person is the person in the mirror. The person in the mirror is your final accountant each and every day of your life. Late at night, when you go into the bathroom and close the door, he is there.

The bad part is, you can't fool the person in the mirror. You can't trick him. It's his judgment and nobody else's that really matters. You can have all the praise of the world. Everybody can say you're a great person; everybody can say nice things about you, but you can't fool the person in the glass.

If you can't look him straight in the eye, you've failed. If you're exactly where you want to be in your life, great. But if you're less than you thought you'd be, less than you planned to be, maybe you don't like him so well. Maybe you avoid looking sometimes because it's too painful.

But when you're there in the bathroom with that person late at night, it doesn't matter what the world says about you. You know what the score really is. You know whether you can look at that person and smile or whether you look and see the man (or woman) who might have been—but wasn't.

Go "do it." You've got nothing to lose and everything to gain. Don't keep holding back thinking you're protecting yourself from disappointment. You're only protecting yourself from life.

Have you ever seen those talk shows where people ask successful people questions? They always ask, "Have you got any regrets in life? If you had your life to live over again, would you do anything differently?"

And almost every one of them says, "No. I'm happy with my life."

Well, I think that's nothing but a lie. When you're growing up, you take everything for granted. Man, if I could go back to when I was fifteen or sixteen, you know what I'd do differently? Just about everything. I'd try harder. I'd pay any price. I'd erase all that fooling around and replace it with the energy and effort and determination that I didn't have then. When I think of how much less I would have had to suffer and let my family suffer, it just about eats me up. I was just playing at life; I wasn't doing all I could do.

Then ten years ago I looked at my life, and it was just a rerun. Each stage had been a repeat of the one before. I was pretty good compared to most people out there, but I didn't want to be a little bit better than most of them. That wasn't what I had planned to do with my life. I wanted to be somebody. I wanted to stand for something. I wanted my life to count for something.

It's tough to see your life frittering away, seeing one thing after another you've tried, thinking this was going to be your thing and all of a sudden discovering it won't work. That's pretty tough to live with.

Then about ten years ago I looked in the mirror at Art Williams, and what I saw made me just a little sick. And I couldn't stand it.

I tried to analyze what I was missing. I said to myself, "Why aren't you succeeding, Art? What's wrong with you, Art? Why are you still just playing around at life?"

I believe with everything that's in me that I didn't work as hard as I could have, believe as much as I could have, because deep down in my heart, I didn't know if Art Williams truly could win. I had never been the best at anything I had ever done, and I think over the years I developed an attitude that said, "I don't know if I'm capable of being somebody. Instead of going out there and giving it everything I've got, I'm going to keep something in reserve and wait for my chance."

Then I got a surprise. I looked up one day ten years ago, and all of a sudden, life was running out.

I made up my mind that I was tired of having regrets. I said to myself, "I don't know if I'm good enough, but this is one time I'm going to stand and fight, show the world that I can give it everything I've got, tell my family and the world to judge me on what I do right now. I'm not going to hold anything back. If I can't do it, then I can stamp myself a failure. I can stamp myself as average and ordinary."

Ten years ago, I made a total commitment, and I went for it.

Now, ten years later, I've become somebody Art Williams is proud of.

You know, most people in business judge you by how much money you make. That's a way to keep score. But there is nothing like feeling good about yourself. I can look at Art Williams and that face in that mirror today and *for the first time in my life,* I like him. I truly like that guy.

I've got more enemies than most of you will ever have. But it doesn't matter what anybody thinks or says about you. The thing that counts is what that person in the mirror says about you.

If there is one piece of advice that I want you to take away from this book, it's this thought: it's time to quit running; it's time to stop hoping for a better situation, a better time, a magic opportunity.

Let me ask you to do something next weekend. Take some time to just sit around and think. Get away for a little while and just think. Think about where you are, where you've been. Make up your mind that you're not going to let anybody or anything tell you that you can't do it. Make up your mind that you're going to go for it. Make up your mind that you're going to be happy, to be positive, to build a better life than you've had in the past. And that you're going to do it *now.* Think about how bad you want to win. Think about the price you're willing to pay. And think about the alternative to winning.

See yourself doing something big again. Dream again. Reach for the stars. Immediately, you'll be set apart from other people—the people who didn't decide to make a difference with their lives.

How many more chances will you have? You know, it's a

shame how much we take life for granted. We think we're invulnerable; we think we've got all the time in the world.

Not true.

My senior year in football I was quarterback, and I broke my left arm in the fifth game of the year. I was despondent. I couldn't believe it.

Before I broke my arm, I thought those Friday nights would go on forever. All of a sudden, my career was over. I didn't have any more chances. What was worse, the team went right on and won without me.

How many more chances will you have to be successful? I believe with everything that's in me that you get more than one chance, but *how many more*? If you don't do it now, what will your future look like? When you look in the mirror five years from now, will your past look exactly the same as it does today?

Think about it long and hard. Quit running; decide to become the person you were meant to be. Go for it. You don't have to do everything perfectly to win. You just have to do all that you can.

Because all you can do is all you can do, but all you can do is *enough*.

A truly inspirational game plan for winning. Refreshing—hard-hitting—challenging! Art Williams' principles of leadership should become the "second Bible" for anyone that desires to do all that he can do!

> Hayden Fry
> *Head Coach, University of Iowa*

With candor and empathy, Art Williams coaches us how to be likable and successful regardless of our past performances. His techniques are dignified by their simplicity.

> Donald W. Zacharias
> *President, Mississippi State University*

This book explains a Winner's philosophy. It contains sound business and motivation principles, simply stated so everyone can understand. Further, these principles are illustrated with numerous vivid and interesting examples which show them Dr. John J. Pepin being implemented. My suggestion: Don't read the book—STUDY IT, chapter by chapter, and incorporate these principles in your personal business philosophy.

> Dr. John J. Pepin
> *Professor of Marketing, Memphis State University;*
> *Professional Marketing and Management Consultant*

Art Williams has done it again. AYCDIAYCD is another exciting and inspirational account of achieving when the odds are long and the world seems a pretty tough place. It has to do with evangelical conviction, belief in one's ability and one's product or service. It is "must reading" for anyone involved in direct marketing. It's a Christian message—about fundamentals, about life, about winning. It's superb!

> William B. Astrop
> *Chairman, Astrop Advisory Corp.*

AYCDIAYCD is a winner! Just like in football, fundamentals are the key to victory in any area of life. And the fundamentals of winning in this book are the best I've seen. I highly recommend this book for anyone who's willing to do what it takes to win!

> Danny Ford
> *Head Football Coach, Clemson University*

Art Williams' proof is in the pudding. Not only is Art Williams a winner, but so are thousands of other people who have followed his principles for winning. I'm motivated to do the same.

> Marvin Arrington
> *President, Atlanta City Council*

There is a growing consensus of opinion that Art Williams could qualify as the Knute Rockne of the insurance industry. Others might compare him to General George S. Patton. Perhaps a combination of the two dynamic personalities would best describe this new, upstart kid in the neighborhood who is taking over and changing the old, traditionally staid block.

Having been a highly talented high-school football coach with a special flair for winning state championships, his talents are now directed toward building a fantastically successful business. Exercising profound leadership and espousing the principles of teamwork, he has recruited some who lacked the athletic ability to have ever won a letter. Many of them have been coached to win and are starters on the A. L. Williams varsity.

If possible to catalog one who lights a spark, kindles the flame of enthusiasm, confidence, spirit, and brings financial gain into a mundane lifestyle, then Art Williams will surely take his place with the great motivational arsonists of all time. His book AYCDIAYCD is an excellent insight into his philosophies.

> Frank "Muddy" Waters
> *Former Head Football Coach, Michigan State University*

Art's approach has proven extraordinarily successful for him and thousands of others in his company, but the fundamentals of success apply to any endeavor. This offers no easy prescription for winning, but rather is based on self-sacrifice, finding a crusade, and uncompromising integrity.

Thomas G. Rosencrants, C.F.A.
Senior Vice President,
Johnson Lane Space Smith & Co., Inc.

Three years ago I became one of the millions who read Art's book *Common Sense* (over 14 million have now been printed), and it changed my life, especially in the financial areas of insurance, retirement, and investments. I have just read AYCDIAYCD and all I can say is, "You've *got* to get a copy of this book. It can change *your* life. The main strengths are: 1. simplicity—everyone can relate, and 2. universality—everyone can be benefited in many areas of their lives."

Dr. Earl Little
President, Christian Law Association; Cofounder,
Christian Legal Defense and Education Foundation

Art has done it again. AYCDIAYCD is an indispensable guide to winning in business and in life. All this from a guy who practices what he preaches and has become one of modern America's most successful entrepreneurs. Thank you Art!

Tom Richter, C.F.A.
Senior Vice President, Robinson Humphrey Co.

For those who have heard Art Williams give a motivational speech and walked away wishing they could capture and share his wit, brilliance, charm, and secret to winning, now they can. Art Williams' new book is must reading for anyone who wants a sure-fire formula for success.

Honorable Pat Swindall
United States Congress

I just read the book from cover to cover and I love it. I'd like for all my friends to read it and practice it. It's real, it's honest, it's practical, and it works. Art expresses a high view of people, and he communicates hope and the possibility of making my life count. I recommend it heartily.

Dr. Ron Jenson
President, High Ground

It's really exciting to see a person, especially a former coach, become a winner because he refused to be average. I've never been around anyone who projects such a positive and winning attitude as Art Williams. I believe he can show you, too, how to become a winner.

Rockey Felker
Head Football Coach, Mississippi State University

After reading the first chapter, I could feel the fire of enthusiasm build. Never before have I read a book that made me want to stand up and tell everybody that I am somebody. Anyone who wants to be a winner should read this book. I am proud to endorse this book as an educator and recommend it to all other professional people.

Cecil C. McDonald
Superintendent of Schools, Cairo, Grady County, Georgia